Luke

A Challenge to Present Theology

EDUARD SCHWEIZER

LUKE

A Challenge
to Present Theology

John Knox Press
ATLANTA

Library of Congress Cataloging in Publication Data

Schweizer, Eduard, 1913-
    Luke, a challenge to present theology.

    Presented as the Thomas White Currie Lectures at the Austin Presbyterian Theological Seminary in January 1980.
    Includes bibliographical references.
    1. Bible. N.T. Luke—Criticism, interpretation, etc. I. Title.

BS2595.2.S33	226'.406	81-85332
ISBN 0-8042-0686-4		AACR2

© copyright John Knox Press 1982
10 9 8 7 6 5 4 3 2 1
Printed in the United States of America
John Knox Press
Atlanta, Georgia 30365

Preface

The Austin Seminary Association and the Board of Trustees of Austin Presbyterian Theological Seminary established a lectureship in 1945 to bring to the seminary campus each year a distinguished scholar to address an annual midwinter convocation of ministers, students, faculty, and other interested people on some phase of Christian thought.

In 1950 the Thomas White Currie Bible Class of the Highland Park Presbyterian Church of Dallas, Texas, undertook the support of this lectureship in memory of the late Dr. Thomas White Currie, founder of the class and third president of the seminary.

In 1980 Eduard Schweizer's name was added to the list of distinguished incumbents of the Currie Lectureship. All who heard him were challenged and inspired as he introduced us afresh to Luke and, through those spectacles, to these times.

We are proud to have sponsored the lectures and now to join with him and John Knox Press in making them available to a wider audience.

Jack Martin Maxwell, President
Austin Presbyterian Theological Seminary

Contents

I.
The Historico-critical Method—
An Avenue to Theological Understanding

In January 1980 I had the honor to deliver the Thomas White Currie Lectures at Austin Presbyterian Theological Seminary. When I got the invitation in the summer of 1979 I immediately knew that I would speak on Luke. This Gospel has intrigued me more and more since I started to work towards the commentary which is to be published by John Knox Press as *The Good News According to Luke.* This small book, which focuses on basic theological questions, emerged. On the one hand, I was constantly harassed by the problems of Christology or soteriology for which Luke seems to have no clear answer. On the other, I detected in an ever-increasing way, to my own surprise, how much his approach helped me to a new theological understanding of the meaning of the Christ event. In some way, it was just the fact that he refrained from giving me a clear-cut statement about the nature or the work of Christ which appealed to me. Instead of that I found a full load of stories about Jesus, of parables, many of them not known to the other evangelists, and of descriptions of different life situations, like that of Jesus' journey to Jerusalem which provided a theologically important new setting of many incidents or sayings.

The Gospel as seen with the eyes of Luke became very human to me. There is much which is left open, unexplained. Rulers like Pilate mingle blood of innocent pilgrims with their sacrifices and towers fall and kill eighteen people who just happened to be on the spot (13:1–5), and there are times in which one should sell one's mantle and buy a sword (22:36). But there is also so much joy to be found throughout this Gospel, and so much trust in the one who cares for the little flock (12:32). There is, perhaps, no really precise theological statement about the salutary effect of Jesus' death. But there is a picture of Jesus as a servant among the disciples, serving them and many others during his whole ministry and up to his death on the cross (22:27).

On the other hand, there is certainly a "divine" side on Luke's portrayal of Jesus. Aren't there too many miracles happening? Does not the resurrected Christ appear with flesh and bones (24:40), even eating broiled fish (24:42–43)? Angels and earthquakes open prisons (Acts 12:10 and 16:26) and the shadow of Peter or the handkerchiefs of Paul heal the sick (Acts 5:15 and 19:12). But Luke knows that prisons are not always opened (Luke 17:25 etc.; Acts 12:2 and 20:22–25). Thus he reminds us of the fact that ordinary or extraordinary happenings in which God succeeds in speaking to us, reaching us, challenging and comforting us, are the real miracles, whether they lead to a visible escape from prison or to suffering and death according to the will of God.

However, is the fact that a Gospel appeals to me in many ways a sufficient reason for accepting it as theological truth? Should I not rather be skeptical, since God's thoughts are not identical with human thoughts? Therefore, just because I am so enormously interested in the theological message of Luke I approach it with a critical mind and a critical method.[1] "Critical" is orginally a Greek word and means nothing else than "distinguishing." When reading the Scripture we must distinguish between the message which should be conveyed to us and the language in which it is conveyed. The Parable of the Prodigal Son contains the remark that the swine which the younger son had to tend were fed with carob bean pods (15:16). We have to distinguish between this statement in itself and its message. If the context were the report of an ancient traveler, the message would probably be a suggestion to the farmers of his home country to try such feeding on their own swine. In the context of the parable of Jesus this is certainly not the point. Its message is the description of the life of the younger son, and whether the hearer feeds his swine, if he has any, with carob bean pods or with any other fodder, is not of the slightest importance. Therefore, our understanding of the Scripture must always and by necessity be a critical understanding.

Yet this created problems time and again. When Martin Luther had translated the Bible, this looked first like a catastrophe. Was this not the end of the unity of the church? There was no longer one generally accepted text. With the Latin text the famous evidence for the doctrine of an original sin disappeared. Romans 5:12 no longer ran "through one man *in* whom all had sinned death spread to all men," but "through one man death spread to all men, *because* all had sinned." And yet how beneficial it was for the whole church that it was forced to rethink its doctrines, to read again and again what the Scripture really said and to ask what its authors wanted to express in their sentences, whether or not it fitted into the patterns of time-honored ways of thinking.

About a century later the writings of Galileo were condemned because they taught a solar system in which the sun was the center and the earth moving around the sun. This seemed to contradict statements like Joshua 10:12 ("Sun, stand thou still at Gibeon"); if the Bible were wrong at one point, marginal as it might be, would not its authority collapse? The issue has been decided long ago, and the church has learned to see that what at first sight seemed to be a catastrophe has become very wholesome for its understanding of God. The scientist has helped the church to fulfill its task and to distinguish between what the Bible wants to proclaim—God's saving acts in the history of Israel—and what it does not want to pro-claim—the laws of physics. The Bible not only lost nothing of its power and authority but even gained new strength, because it be-came much clearer what this book really wants to tell us. Since the time of honest discussion between natural science and theology it has become obvious that it is no longer possible to read the Bible in a detached way like a textbook in physics, just looking for some new information about interesting facts, but that one must read it with the expectation and the readiness to get personally involved.

New problems came up when scholars learned to take the dif-ferent variants of manuscripts seriously. The only passage in the Testament in which the trinitarian dogma could be found explicitly (1 John 5:7–8) proved to be a late addition in Latin translations. Therefore Luther had already excluded this passage in his transla-tion, but it was reprinted in most editions of the New Testament for a long time, until it became definitely clear that it did not belong to the original text. Other changes which were made during the process of tradition, like the gloss about fasting in Mark 9:29, were eventu-ally detected. Thus not even the text in its original language was a totally safe basis of truth. And again, what looked like a disaster led to a very fortunate development. Since one could no longer find the trinitarian formula in the Scripture, the church was obliged to re-think its belief in the triune God in the light of passages like Matthew 28:19 or 1 Corinthians 12:3–5.

More decisive was the end of all dreams about a unique and holy biblical language. For many centuries no Hebrew writings were known except the Old Testament, and the Greek of the New Testament was so very different from that of Plato and Plutarch that scholars thought of a specifically holy language, given by God himself, because no human tongue would be able to express the mysteries of God and his salvation. Then Deissmann detected the papyri and potsherds on which ordinary people wrote their notes and short letters, and their language was very much like that of the New Testament. Again, many great constructions of theologians had to fall. There was no miraculous speech in which God's mysteries could be captivated, no heavenly language in which humanity could get hold of God's nature and work. Once more this seemingly negative insight proved to become a real liberation to new revelations. It was no longer possible to speak of God in a foreign angelic language, as for instance in the Latin of the mass. It became an urgent task of the church "to watch the mouth of ordinary people," as Luther formulated it, to express the truth in their words. Slowly, the church understood that its proclamation made sense only if expressed in words and sentences which were used in everyday life and were, therefore, understandable. To be sure, the proclamation of the gospel became much more difficult, since one could no longer recite Latin formulas or repeat pious clichés. But the church was urged to combine its words and phrases with clear concepts, and this saved it from spiritual freezing and dying.

This meant that it was no longer so easy to understand the Bible literally. One had to know first what a word actually meant in the time in which it was written, and this often required a long and troublesome research before one could repeat it in modern language. This was an insight that one could have had already in the time of Luther. He was perplexed because he read the Bible literally. He interpreted the "justice of God" as anyone in his time would have interpreted this term until he realized that the Hebrew term did not mean the distributory "justice," rewarding the good and punishing the bad, but described the unique "righteousness of God" which fights for the weak, helps the poor, exalts the lowly, justifies the sinner. But even then the debate went on. Catholics thought that such an interpretation would destroy the seriousness of conversion and of a life in faith, and Lutherans doubled back by even condemning all good works. It is a fruit of careful scholarly investigation that the double aspect of the righteousness of God as gift for and as power in humanity has been seen in the last decades by both Catholic and Protestant theologians.

Stiffnecked opposition arose when the authenticity of some writings of the Old or New Testament were attacked. If it was no longer sure that a letter or a book written, according to its own testimony, by an apostle or a prophet really came from his pen, was this not the end of all biblical authority? Again the Scripture shone in new and strong light as soon as teachers of the church accepted this truth without anxiety. Among the marvelous commentaries of Adolf Schlatter, for instance, the one on the Pastoral epistles is perhaps the least helpful, just because he continually wants to prove its Pauline character. There are certainly reminiscences of Paul and even Pauline formulations, but on the whole they look rather like writings of an old and lame apostle if compared with his earlier letters. But the same would happen if we compared a modern theologian and his message merely with one of his predecessors in order to find out how much his theology was exactly the same as that of the predecessor. As soon as one is freed from this idea and no longer thinks that the Pastoral epistles should simply say the same as Paul, one detects a totally different situation in the background of the churches of that time with different problems and, therefore, also different answers. When scholars realized that these writings came from another pen and were written in another time, they realized how illuminating they were, because they dealt with problems that are much closer to our own world and to the situation of our church today than the authentic epistles of Paul.

But was it not different with form-criticism? Was this not an attack against the very substance of the gospel? If the events reported in our gospels did not happen in the way in which they were narrated there—or even not happen at all—was this not the end of faith? If some of the stories were nothing but the creation of the post-Easter church, stemming from its discussion with rabbis or un-believers of its time, are they still the revelation of God's *heilsge-schichte*? It is impossible to deal with these problems at some length. It may suffice, for the moment, to state that, again, the church was highly furthered in its knowledge of God's will by these new in-sights. More and more, we understood that the evangelists did not want to be historians in the modern sense of the word, only interest-ed in accumulating facts, but were witnesses who testify to the truth of God's presence in Jesus, which cannot simply be proved or dis-proved by historical facts. If we had a sound film of the newsreel of Jerusalem showing the crucifixion of Jesus, it would certainly teach us some interesting details and perhaps even record some words of Jesus that we do not yet know. However, it would not tell us what really happened. We should know then how Jesus looked, and we should find him sympathetic or, perhaps, repelling. We should get the idea that this was an innocent man or, perhaps, just the contra-ry. We should hear some words of his and be moved by them or, perhaps, not at all. But we should, in all this, not realize what hap-pened. This can only be told by the evangelist who understood in his faith that it was indeed God himself who acted in this event. He has no proof for this his understanding, except the proof of the Spir-it and the power of God which is at work in his words. But it is this Spirit of God alone who can really show us what happened in this crucifixion.

Two passages may illustrate what is implied here. Mark 15:25 reports that Jesus was crucified at nine A.M., John 19:14 that he was sentenced at twelve noon. Historically speaking, we can only state that at least one of the evangelists must err, or we should have to try a rather desperate solution and assume that John had used a totally different system of counting the hours of the day which is not known to us from other sources. But if we do so, in order to save a historical reliability of the Bible which would not allow any discrep-ancy, we cease to read it humbly, and we deprive ourselves of hear-ing its message. For, why is it important to Mark to state this hour of the crucifixion? The message that he wants to convey to us is, strictly speaking, not the fact that it was nine A.M. when Jesus was crucified. This is in itself of no importance for our faith and our salvation. What he wanted to express by this remark was, first, the truth that it was God's will which dominated all the events of this day. In a rhythm of three hours the day ran from the crucifixion in the third hour to the beginning of the darkness in the sixth and to the death of Jesus in the ninth. Second, it was probably already to his source very important that in this way Amos 8:9 has been fulfilled: "And on that day, says the Lord GOD, I will make the sun go down at noon, and darken the earth in broad daylight." This means the message of this passage is neither nine A.M. nor twelve noon, but the coming of the day of the Lord as prophesied by Amos. The death of Jesus as the judgment of God, foretold by all the prophets, is actually the content of that reference to day and hour in Mark. This is true whether it really happened in exactly this hour or not. Referring to the noon hour is the language in which Mark—or rather his source—expressed the theological truth of Jesus' crucifixion as being the fulfillment of all the hopes of Israel.

Why is it important to John to know that Jesus was condemned at noon to the death penalty? This becomes clear when we see that he dates the crucifixion on the day before the passover (18:28; 19:14), whereas the Synoptists date it on the passover itself. According to 19:36 it is very important to John that "these things (witnessed by one who was present, vs. 35) took place that the scripture might be fulfilled, 'Not a bone of him shall be broken.' " This is what Exodus 12:46 says of the passover lamb. John has begun his Gospel by pointing to "the Lamb of God, who takes away the sin of the world" (1:29). He ends it by pointing to the one who dies exactly in the hour in which the passover lambs are slaughtered, in the afternoon of the day before passover. Thus, again, the message of John is not the hour of twelve o'clock noon, but the truth that in Jesus all the sacrifices of the passover lambs have found their definite fulfillment: "Behold, the Lamb of God, who takes away the sin of the world." And again this is true, irrespective of the hour of the historical crucifixion of Jesus.

Thus what Mark and John want to express is the meaning of

the death of Jesus for the reader, as the fulfillment of the prophecies about the coming day of the Lord and as the definite sacrifice of the passover lamb. And yet they do not simply couch this truth in a dogmatic formula like "the death of Jesus is the sacrifice for the sin of the world, which fulfills the Old Testament." They narrate the events of Good Friday. They proclaim the death of Jesus, which implies both the report of an event that has happened within earthly history and the preaching of its meaning for the hearer. This double aspect of the Gospel is the problem with which we have to wrestle in the following chapters.

The same problem arises in a much more disquieting way when we look at the Easter events. Whether Jesus was crucified at nine A.M. or around two P.M. is of little importance, and nobody doubts that he was really crucified. This is different with the resurrection. A critical investigation of the texts showed that, of all the appearances which are reported in 1 Corinthians 15:5–8, only the one before the twelve is narrated in the Gospel (Luke 24:34 is no narrative), and the reports even contradict each other. According to Luke, the risen Lord appeared to his disciples on Easter Sunday and told them to stay in Jerusalem up to the time of Pentecost. According to Matthew, the first appearance took place in Galilee, and, since some of the disciples were still doubting, it must have been the first one. Moreover, the narrative of the Jerusalem appearances in John is totally different from that of Luke. It is certain that Cephas and the twelve, the more than five hundred brethren, James and all the apostles, and finally Paul himself (1 Cor. 15:5–8) were convinced they had seen the risen Lord.[2] But who knows whether it was not merely a vision or a hallucination? And since one tradition was only interested in what probably was the first appearance (that on the Galilean mountain), another one only in the Jerusalem appearances (which probably happened after the return of the disciples to the city), we do not even know when and where these men saw the risen Lord. Is this not the end of all faith?

Again, what seemed to be a total disaster proved to be very helpful. It was just the historico-critical approach which clarified what faith really is. It is certainly not identical with an orthodoxy that takes some facts for granted. There were, according to Mark,

orthodox believers who recognized very early in the ministry of
Jesus that he was the son of God—the demons (Mark 3:11; 5:7).
Even Peter, who did not quite reach the same grade of orthodox
belief but realized at least that Jesus was the Christ, was rebuked
some minutes later because it became quite clear that he did not
know at all what he had said (Mark 8:29–33). Thus an indubitable
proof of a miraculous event would not have changed the lives of the
disciples. The discovery of the empty tomb did not create faith
(with the possible exception of John 20:8), it was the word of the
risen Lord which ordered the disciples to return to the city and to
proclaim his lordship, though this might lead them into prison and
even death. Thus they were not simply assured of the possibility of
miracles; the fact of the resurrection of Jesus did not become a
guarantee of their own resurrection after death. They were, primarily, sent out again and in an even more demanding way than during
the earthly ministry of Jesus. "The cause of Jesus went on." The
band of Galilean men who had fled so that not one of them was
ready to care for the burial of Jesus was transformed by the word of
the risen Lord to an enthusiastic group of messengers of his lordship
ready to go to prison and to death. Even the resurrection of Jesus
was not simply a fact to be accepted as true, but rather the proclamation of the power of God which comforted and challenged the
disciples and changed their lives. Does this mean that the fact itself
is of no importance, that it is only its meaning for the disciples and
their attitudes to life that counts, as it was with the dating of the
crucifixion in Mark 15:25 and John 19:14? But again this is only
half of the truth. It was the same historico-critical method that
showed how much the first disciples understood Easter in apocalyptic terms. Since the resurrection of the dead was expected at the end
of the times, they understood, first of all, Jesus' resurrection as the
beginning of the end of the world, probably expecting the final resurrection of all the dead within a very short time in Jerusalem.
Therefore, they left their properties and homes and moved with
their families to Jerusalem. Texts like Matthew 27:51–53 still show
something of these expectations: ". . . and the earth shook, and the
rocks were split; the tombs also were opened, and many bodies of
the saints who had fallen asleep were raised, and coming out of the

tombs." Christian prophets must have played an important role in
the earliest church in Jerusalem because all prophets mentioned in
Acts are people who came either from Jerusalem or at least from
Palestine. Thus the Jerusalem congregation was, as far as we can
see, a very enthusiastic group, full of apocalyptic hopes and expecting the end of the world.

This may look very strange to us, and we cannot simply revive
that kind of faith. But it shows how much the resurrection of Jesus
was, for that first group of believers, the beginning of a new world.
It was most certainly not merely something which happened in the
hearts of some pious followers of Jesus; it was a very objective new
creation, the onset of the new earth under a new heaven. Whether it
began in Galilee or in Jerusalem or in both places (there with the
twelve, there with the women and the two men on the road to Emmaus) did not matter.

But it was of first importance that it did start here and now, in
the new life of the church, in the proclamation of the gospel, in the
manifestations of the power of God's Spirit, and that there was the
promise of a final fulfillment on the last day. It was therefore never
a very central problem that the parousia did not happen soon; the
new world was, in some way, already present, as the kingdom of
God had been present in the days of the earthly Jesus. Thus, again,
both aspects of faith were united. The proclamation of the resurrection of Jesus was both an appeal which changed the life of the
church and a report of God's mighty deeds, which were the basis of
this new life.

Love dies if a husband inhibits all irritation, represses, often
unconsciously, all doubts about his wife, and adores an idealistic
picture of her which is not actually herself, because he grooms an
idol and not his real spouse. Love also dies if a husband looks for
indubitable proof of his wife, for instance, by watching her through
a private eye. Even if the reports were all blameless, this would
never be the beginning of real love but its end. And yet love needs
visible and audible and palpable manifestations of love within the
"history" of a marriage. It even lives by these manifestations. They
are never unambiguous, and one could always explain them in a
different way, but they nurture the mutual love, though only those

who already are loving can interpret them with total certainty as love-signs.

In the same way faith dies if it ceases to think and even to doubt, if it represses all questions and adores an idealistic picture of the Bible or of Christ himself, an idol instead of the real Scripture and the real living Lord. It dies also if it bases itself on indubitable proof which it wants to get in an objective way without getting involved. And yet faith needs all the manifestations of God's love in the history of humanity, which are never unambiguous and yet lead to experiences of the reality of this love of God. Therefore it needs the witnesses of the New Testament who testify to the truth of these manifestations and of their own experiences.

Does historico-critical research lead to the truth without erring? It goes without saying that this is not so. Anyone can point to grave mistakes. But, by and large, it corrected itself time and again if it was an honest critical research, not biased by dogmatic presuppositions. Is historico-critical research not dangerous? It certainly is. But harmless repetition of long approved statements has never helped. The church has to dare to proclaim the truth in the language of its time or to refrain from saying anything. Can historico-critical research create faith? Certainly not. Faith is always the gift of God himself. But it can open the way to real listening, to an openness which does not adore a self-made image of God and his word but exposes itself to the living word of God, which threatens all our own ideas and theological constructions, but just so frees us from ourselves to the experience of the living and loving God. This is the point where we have reached the limits of all historico-critical methods. It is the point on which the object of our research must become the subject and start to speak to us. It is the moment of "perception" to which all scholarly research must lead.

This is very similar to what a scientist may also experience. He may weigh and measure and photograph his object for a long time; but real discoveries are made when the "object" becomes in some way "subject" and starts to speak to the research worker. He may see a piece of rock, and suddenly that rock starts to pose questions: "Why is it possible that these two geological layers are mingled here?" If this starts a process of thinking in the brain of the investigator—"Why have I never seen that? What does it mean? How is this to be explained? What is the reason for this strange fact?"—then real progress is made. All the measuring and weighing can only lead to this moment of insight. Sometimes, it would not even be necessary for a specific individual to have personally gone through all the measuring and weighing, though real progress is unthinkable without all the experiments which lead to the right questions and confirm the right answers.

Thus we are back to the problem of what history means for faith. Historico-critical methods are certainly not necessary for the salvation of the individual believer. But if we prohibited them or limited their functions anxiously, we would forget that God became incarnate in the earthly history of a man, called Jesus of Nazareth. If, on the other hand, we thought that historico-critical research were just everything and the only basis of faith, we would forget that it was God who became flesh in this history.

On the following pages I try to find my way between the two extremes. The following four chapters contain the Currie Lectures, to which I have added the footnotes and the final chapter. What I try to do comes out of a deep concern. The church urgently needs those who are ready to do all the historico-critical work that has to be done. It needs, at the same time, equally urgently (or even more urgently) those who are open to the gift of faith. If we condemn each other, if some are not ready to give to scholars the freedom to do their work and also to err, and if others do not respect the deepness of faith of those who cannot always follow them, the church falls apart. The gifts of God are different, as different as 1 Corinthians 12 depicts them, but the church needs all of his gifts; otherwise it dies. God may grant us to become more and more his people in which every member knows how much it needs the other ones.

II.
The Continental Background
of Modern Theology

When we try to look forward to what modern theology should achieve we have to see whence we came, where we are, and whither we shall go. Hence, I'll try to draw the picture, as I personally see it, of what has happened in Continental-European theology, whether in consequent or inconsequent development of earlier positions. This certainly means drawing a very condensed and therefore by necessity simplifying sketch of this development, for which I apologize sincerely. I am quite aware of the fact that the scholars of whom I shall speak saw the dangerous points in their systems and tried to shield them against misunderstandings. We should keep this definitely in mind lest the sketch becomes a caricature. Also I shall not deal with American and British theological designs but exceptionally, simply because I am certainly no expert in this field, whereas, being a Swiss, I may know something of the theological movements on our continent from the days of my studies in Switzerland and Germany in 1932–36 up to today. German theologians seem to be quoted more often than others. If this is true, perhaps this story I heard explains why: Once at the entry of heaven there was a door with the inscription "Heaven," and plenty of people pressed to enter there, but there was also a second door labeled "Lectures About Heaven," and most of the Germans ran to this room. What I propose to do now is to look a bit through this second door in order to learn from Luke, step by step, to turn to the first one.

1. From Harnack and Blumhardt
to K. Barth and R. Bultmann

At the beginning of this century the lecture theater was dominated by *Adolf von Harnack*, for whom "God and the immortal worth of the human soul" was the center of all theological thinking. Something like this was to be expected in consequence of Hegel's philosophy in which God was the spirit that manifested itself increasingly in history, history being the progressive development of the human mind. This was German idealism: God was to be found in the higher realms of human ideas, in the ideal world as conceived by thinkers, poets, and artists. Jesus was, according to such theology, the one who had brought a new experience of God and had revealed the infinite value of the human soul, which, for Harnack, was more or less the same as the human reasoning mind. From other pulpits men like *Christoph Blumhardt, Jr.* and *Leonhard Ragaz* taught. The former was a well-known pastor in southern Germany and member of the then radical Socialist Party, the second a professor of systematic theology in Zurich, Switzerland, pacifist, conscientious objector, and also a socialist. For them the social engagement for the betterment of the position of the working class was *the* focal point of all theology. This was the new Hegel, as interpreted by Karl Marx and his followers. History, according to them, was totally shaped by economic problems. In contrast to a flight into the ideal realms of human thoughts, they called humanity back to the real world of labor and wages, money investments and economic power, industrial and social development. Jesus, then, was the one who had, as a social reformer, taken the part of the poor and dispossessed.[3] For both wings of theological teaching, it was the earthly Jesus who had been teacher and example either of a revaluation of the human soul and its religious or philosophical thinking or of a new assessment of social activity.

When I came as a freshmen to the university, the situation had totally changed. *Albert Schweitzer* had put an end to those dreams. A reconstruction of a life of Jesus was, according to him, impossible.

> The material with which it has hitherto been usual to solder the sections together in a life of Jesus will not stand the temperature test. Exposed to the cold air of critical scepticism it cracks; when the furnace of eschatology is heated to a certain point the solderings melt. In both cases the sections all fall apart. Formerly it was possible to book through-tickets at the supplementary psychological-knowledge office which enabled those travelling in the interest of Life-of-Jesus construction to use express trains, thus avoiding the inconvenience of having to stop

at every little station, change and run the risk of missing their connection. This ticket office is now closed. There is a station at the end of each section of the narrative, and the connections are not guaranteed.[4]

This was the situation into which *Karl Barth's* trumpet blast exploded. The Word of God coming vertically from above became the new tune of the twenties and thirties,[5] when Barth, born 1886, taught as Professor of Systematic Theology first in Münster then in Bonn and Basel.

The difficulty of his position was what some later called his "positivism of revelation," which means his view of the Bible as a direct and objective revelation of God. However, to accept it without understanding of what one accepted would certainly not be faith, but rather something like learning a magical, totally incomprehensible formula in the belief that its recitation would heal or even save eternally. However, if human understanding of the biblical message is relevant, what is the relation between the biblical truth, as laid down in the Scripture, and our assumption of it? Must we simply accept that we are saved by the death of Christ? Or is it important that we understand this in such a way? And if so, what is the relation of the saving event of the death of Christ and our understanding of it?

These are the questions which plagued *Rudolf Bultmann*, born 1884, since 1921 Professor of New Testament in Marburg, Germany. It was a terrible shock for many of his colleagues, including A. von Harnack, that this radically critical interpreter joined the new group of dialectic theology.[6] He was one with Karl Barth in the belief that Jesus was not interesting for theology as a human teacher or example, but only as the Christ, the Word of God to all people of all ages. Therefore it was his resurrection which interpreted definitely what his life and his death really meant. Albert Schweitzer had shown that the Gospels had been written in the light of Easter; hence it was, according to Bultmann, theologically not necessary to try to go behind this Easter belief. If one did so, as he himself had done, one would merely detect a Jewish prophet whose teaching and acting was that of an Old Testament figure.[7] This is of some interest because it is the immediate preparation of the Easter belief, but not basically different from Jewish and Hellenistic ideas which also form some preparatory basis to this belief. Bultmann did not deny that there was some continuity between Jesus and the post-Easter Christ, but the decisive fact that distinguished Jesus Christ from all other prophets was the Easter-event, that means the insight of the church that he was *the* Word of God, reconciling the world to him. Jesus has risen into the proclamation of the kerygma.[8]

Even then the difference between the two was perceptible. If someone had asked Karl Barth: When were you converted? he could have answered: On Good Friday, 30 A.D. (or whatever year it was). Rudolf Bultmann would have replied: When I first understood the doctrine of justification, maybe in reading Luther's commentary on Romans or listening to the lectures of his teacher Hermann or whenever this may have happened. For Barth, it was the act of God in the crucifixion and resurrection of Jesus Christ that was decisive, though it was doubtless important to understand this in order to lead a life in gratitude towards God. For Bultmann, the change in understanding oneself, as given by the message of justification by faith, was the decisive event, though he emphasized that that was always a gift of God from "outside of ourselves" and not possible without the Christ-event.

His marvelous contribution to the history of theology in our century was his combination of honest scholarly criticism and deep devotion to a saving faith.[9] It was the critical student of the New Testament who detected that the Gospels were not interested in all the historical details but in the call to the reader to hear the word of God spoken to him or her *in* this or that story, *in* this or that parable of Jesus, comprehensively in the totality of the life, death, and resurrection of Jesus Christ. The presupposition of this existential approach is the basic sameness of humanity throughout the centuries. Bultmann knows, of course, about essential changes in human cultures and philosophies, and he takes them seriously. As a marvelous exegete of the New Testament, he has pointed to the transformation of the gospel from its Palestinian-Jewish origins to the new forms in which Hellenistic communities had to express it. But this does not affect the truth that the basic problems and possibilities of people remain the same, even if they manifest themselves in different ways in their respective cultural backgrounds. Whatever and whenever they live, people search, in a thousand different ways, to confirm themselves, to justify themselves. Thus, wherever and whenever they live, people need the gospel of the one God who, in Jesus Christ, confirms and justifies them by grace, not on the basis of the works that they are able to perform.

However, if it is the insight in the message of justification by faith which saves people, why do they need more than this message? Is the so-called Christ-event more than its historical source, and could we today not dispense with this source? Would not a philosophy of existentialism lead us to the same change of our self-understanding, as long as it stressed the character of gift of all human existence? This has happened to the Pauline message in gnosticism. The Christ-myth has been replaced by the Attis- or Osiris-myth or any of the ancient myths which defined human existence as a divine gift, or even better: as of divine origin, so that the myth, and the message of the gnostic philosopher who interprets it, must merely remind him or her of what he or she had forgotten. Bultmann saw the difference between the philosopher and the theologian in their understanding of sin. Humans are, according to the New Testament, sinners in their very being; that means: even in their piety—or better: exactly in their piety—they still live for themselves, for their own glory, their own greatness. Therefore, nothing short of the life and death of Jesus Christ can free them from their desire in which all human life is rooted. I asked Bultmann when I was a student in Marburg whether, in this case, the Christ-event was more than the motive which moved me to change my understanding of life, and he finally agreed, after some discussion, with this term of "motive."

2. The Bultmannians and Barthians

This proved to be the dangerous point. For *Herbert Braun,* born 1903, Professor of New Testament in Berlin and Mainz after World War II, it is exactly the understanding of human existence which forms the only constant content of the different New Testament books, whereas the teaching about Christ is variable. Anthropology, not Christology, is what the New Testament tries to teach. God, as he reveals himself in Jesus Christ, is, therefore, identical with the event of liberation of people from their wrong understanding of themselves as being root and goal of their lives, to the new insight in the givenness of their lives. Thus, God, as he can be experienced by us, is, still according to Braun, the "I shall" and "I may love (my fellow-man)." [10] In a similar way, *Will Marxsen*, born 1919, Professor of New Testament in Bethel in 1956, five years later in Münster, Germany, deals with the resurrection of Jesus Christ. Again, it is the question of what it means to the hearer of the message. For Marxsen, it is the encounter of the risen Lord with the disciples which is important. Whether, as Jews, they interpret it as resurrection, or, as Greeks, as the continuing life of Jesus' immortal soul, or, as people today, as the fact that "the cause of Jesus goes on," is irrelevant.[11] This is but different interpretations of the same faith, and an ecumenical approach will not stop at these variants but will see the fundamental one belief. The risen Christ is Jesus, as he lives on in his disciples. There is no doubt that Marxsen wants to emphasize that it is God as revealed in Jesus' life and death, and not merely human idealism, that lives in the disciples who get engaged in this "cause of Jesus." And yet the difference between the New Testament message and Marxsen, for whom resurrection is but one interpretation among others of the continuing influence of Jesus, is, it seems to me, a real one. It is the difference between saying, for instance to a dying friend: *"Your cause* will go on; what you have strived for will live on in our engagement in the same fight"–or saying: *"You* will live on in a life with God which is the fulfillment of all earthly striving and, therefore, the goals for which you are striving will remain in God's good hands." Again, there is no doubt that the former interpretation is an enormously important part of the truth; but would it still be the truth without the latter one?

Neither is it the full truth without the first answer, and we shall listen with open minds to this question put by Braun and Marxsen. But if our charity or our engagement in the cause of Jesus, even when essentially understood as a gift, becomes *the* interpretation of God, are we not back to pagan idolatry? Love is a gift which people experience in their lives. Therefore, the Greeks called it "God": Eros or Aphrodite. It is a progress, when we speak in this context of agape, of charity, rather than of sexual desire, but is it so enormously different? We know that there is some sexual component even in the most unselfish love and that sexual love without some unselfishness, some focusing on the *thou*, is no love at all. Hence, I fear we are back to the human m: ıd, back to what Calvin called "a factory of idols."

It was *Ernst Käsemann*, born 1906, Professor of New Testament in Mainz, Göttingen, and Tübingen, who, as a former disciple of Bultmann, called his colleagues back to history in a famous paper read at a meeting of the Old Marbugians. History, as the "text," has priority over its theological interpretation. He understands history, especially that of the earthly Jesus, in the apocalyptic way of the Bible as the road of God into the future, leading from creation to fulfillment. Thus, apocalypticism is, in the New Testament, the "mother of theology."[12] Recently, *Pierre Gisel*, born 1947, professor of systematic theology in the French-speaking part of Switzerland, has analyzed in a philosophically well-founded book of some 700 pages Käsemann's understanding of history and the problem of the necessary conflict between history and truth.[13] On the Catholic side, *Xavier Leon-Dufour*, Jesuit and professor of New Testament in Paris, understands resurrection primarily as an act of God which, by necessity, has to be proclaimed in form of narrative.[14] This is very helpful, perhaps more than his suggestion to see the person of the risen Lord as being one with the universe personified in him. All this leads back to the Barthians.

Among them, *Gerhard von Rad*, born 1901, Professor of Old Testament in Jena 1934, Göttingen in 1945 and Heidelberg in 1949, took up Barth's position in an unusually fruitful way. God, he taught, is not to be found in speculative thoughts and high ideas but in his acts in the history of Israel. It is in his deeds, often ambiguous, often correcting former experiences, often changing fixed views of earlier prophets, even biblical authors, that we find him.[15] *Wolfhart Pannenberg*, born 1928, Professor of Systematic Theology in Wuppertal, Mainz, and Munich since 1958, made the next step. If God is manifest in history, then too in the universal history. Of course, we cannot see him directly in the course of all history. This we shall only do when looking back from the point of fulfillment on the last day. However, in Jesus, the coming kingdom of God has

already broken into our time. Thus those who have learned to see
Jesus as the revelation of God will see God's paces in history, also
outside of the church.[16] There was but one more step to go in order
to be back to the factory of idols. As soon as God's manifestation in
the history of Jesus was identified with social engagement, new
standings arose. *Jürgen Moltmann*, born 1926, Professor of Systematic Theology in Wuppertal, Bonn, and Tübingen since 1958 (and
others less cautiously) argued that God was again not much more
than human love. It was corporate love instead of individual love;
but again, human activity took the place of God. By this we simply
come back to the beginning of this century, to Harnack's immortal
soul and its ability of loving and to Blumhardt's social engagement.
Is theology to be reduced to anthropology? The new dogmatic of
Gerhard Ebeling, Professor of Systematic Theology in Tübingen and
Zurich, born 1912, deals wisely with that question in the wake of
existential theology.

3. Neopositivism and *heilsgeschichte*

Before trying to look for new ways, two extreme positions
must be mentioned. In protest against existential interpretation,
neopositivists declare that all statements which cannot be verified
or falsified, like "Jesus has risen from the dead" or "his death on the
cross is the reconciliation of the world," are senseless.[17] Some of
them are longing for a safe basis of faith in indubitable facts which
do not depend on always questionable interpretations. But *Hans
Küng*, born 1928 in Switzerland, since 1960 Catholic professor of an
ecumenical chair in Tübingen University, has rightly objected that
the very basis of the approach is impossible. Its main statement
is, in and of itself, senseless, since it can neither be verified nor falsified that there is something like "sense," and if there is, what it
is.[18] *Ebeling* emphasizes that the coming into being of our earth
can be analyzed by way of verification and falsification of different hypotheses, but that there is also a meaning of this process
for human life. A scientist who would never question what the results of his investigations mean for us and our way of life would
certainly not be a good scientist. The responsibility of humanity for the not limitless life of nature cannot be verified or falsi-

fied, but is a truth, not less important than the finds of modern science.[19]

On the other side of the spectrum we find the view of *heilsgeschichte* as presented by *Karl Rahner,* born 1904, Catholic Professor of Systematic Theology in Innsbruck, Munich, and Münster. Like Bultmann, he starts from the human existence which "transcends" itself. This means: The human mind differs from the instinct of the animals in the desire to ask questions. It knows of human limits and it is driven to inquire after the beyond. This is what Rahner calls the human "anonymous" knowledge of God as source and aim of existence. Bultmann had spoken of the *"vorverstandnis,"* the "pre-comprehension." As somebody who has no friend knows in some way what a friend is, but knows really only when he or she has found a friend, so people know in some way who God is, though they only start to know truly when they have been given to believe in him. From this starting point, Rahner goes on a totally different road. This "unconscious" knowledge of God is, for Rahner, an objective proof of a process in which life develops from mere matter to vegetation, to animal life of increasingly higher forms, and finally to human beings, from the first ape-like man to his figure of today. In Jesus Christ the god-man has appeared, in whom the final goal of all human development has been anticipated. He is the guarantee of what all humanity will reach in the end. Compared with the millions of years of evolution, the period of humankind, especially from Abraham to the parousia, is but one short and last phase. As the figure of Jesus Christ shows the final aim of God, so there is, like a frame of this picture, in the Old Testament and in the church history the "official, churchly (*kirchenhafte*), pure" *heilsgeschichte.*[20]

Rahner takes up ideas uttered first by *Teilhard de Chardin,* born 1899, natural scientist and Catholic philosopher, who understands nature, in the wake of Darwinism, but in a totally reverted view as evolution towards the point Omega (biblically the kingdom of God). In some way, this is Hegel's view of history as manifestation of God, but based on science, not an idealistic pattern filled "from above," but rather a theory built "from below." While Teilhard starts from science, nourished by his Catholic faith, Rahner bases his view on the Scripture seen in the light of modern science. The Augustinian separation of grace and nature can no longer be kept. The world is not to be identified with God, but it is in it that God's grace manifests itself. History of the world and *heilsgeschichte* are not identical, since human sin causes interferences (like a thunderstorm on a TV program), but they are coexistent.

Is such a position possible? Can we apply the evolution of nature as seen by Darwin as a model of the evolution of humanity as seen by the Bible to which the survival of the weak (and not of the strong!) is so important? Is not human sin a factor which alters the parallels between nature in general and humanity? According to Genesis 1–3 evolution leads us from a high level in paradise to a very low level, and all apocalyptic texts of the Old and the New Testament speak of deterioration of humanity and nature towards the end. "In the lasts days there will come times of stress . . . men will be lovers of self, . . . inhuman, . . . haters of good" (2 Tim. 3: 1–4). Can a history in which the cross of Golgotha forms the center be understood as evolution from low beginnings to ever higher goals?

Thus an extreme Protestant position calls into question everything except facts that can be verified by scientific methods. An extreme Catholic position presupposes that grace perfects nature in an evolution towards the unity of humanity and God. Is one unable to recognize God or does one always know about him, though not explicitly? Both ways, especially the work of Rahner, have helped the progress of theological thinking enormously. Yet they do not really solve the problems.

4. Modern approaches

What then? There seems to be one point of consensus between such different theologians as Rahner, Moltmann, Küng, Schillebeeckx, and Jüngel. It is the understanding of God as a *living* God. The patristic theology distinguished sharply between an immanent (or essential) trinity and an economic trinity. The latter term described the three "persons" of the trinity, Father, Son, and Spirit, as three different ways in which God manifested himself in the course of the *heilsgeschichte,* in creation as the Father of all beings, in the ministry of Jesus as the Son, in his work on our hearts as the Spirit. These are in this view three different aspects of God's action. God is not Father, Son, and Spirit aside from his acts. So we may say of an older friend: "Without being related to me, he acted as a father." Immanent trinity stresses the unchanging trinitarian being of God. In and of himself, not merely when acting in creation, redemption, or sanctification, he is Father, Son, and Spirit. Behind this distinction lies a real and essential problem, to which we shall come back. Nonetheless, is it really sustainable? Can we speak or think of a God who is not an *acting*—and this means a *living* !—God, without replacing God by a dead idol? Is such a distinction not merely a result of Greek or Western thinking? A European or North-American child is asked at school a thousand times: "What is this?" It may be a flower, a piece of rock, a geometric figure, a difficult form of a Latin verb, even a poem or a painting whose creator is hidden from the class. A Hebrew or an Oriental teacher would only very rarely ask "What is this" but rather ask: "What has happened? What did he do? Who did that?" The teacher has told the children numerous stories and is not interested in an abstract being, an unchanging essence but is interested in the acts of the heavenly or earthly beings or things that encounter people. When the author of Job 40–41 sees the hippopotamus,"which makes his tail stiff like a cedar," and the crocodile, out of whose mouth "go flaming torches, sparks of fire leap forth," out of whose nostrils "comes forth smoke as from a boiling pot," he adores God who acts in such a surprising way that he creates so unthinkably strange creatures. A Greek might also have adored God when seeing these two beasts but only after having dissected them and having found exactly the same system of blood circulation as in the body of a mouse in his native country. Thus the Hebrew adores the act of the living God who, at his will, may create the strangest beings, while the Greek adores the unchanging divine rules and systems that he or she detects behind the various faces of the different earthly beings.

When speaking of the God of the Bible, should we not start from an Old Testament background? If there are unchangeable rules and systems—within some limits!—they are the seal of the creator and not laws which shape and bind him. He is not subject to these laws but is their source. He is the living God, free to act as he wills. Therefore it is impossible to define once for all who God is except by saying how he has acted, how he acts today, and how he will act in conformity with his promises. It is his *existence,* which means his life, his acting, which is his essence. There is no abstract, theoretical essence of God beside his existence, his acts. Therefore the economic trinity—God acting in history as Father, Son, and Spirit—is identical with his very being, the immanent or essential trinity. Even if we speak of a friend, we can, of course, indicate some more or less unchanging items: male, height 1.80 meters, eyes blue. But even his height or the color of his eyes may change, and, at any rate, by giving these qualifications we have not really described him. He actually is what he lives, and though there is some continuity, this changes with each minute. We may speak of his sense of humor, which may become true today or tomorrow again, or of his deep seriousness, which may prove itself next week, etc. We may expect rightly to see all this when meeting him, but we have to wait for it. We cannot detect it in the same way as we test his height by simply applying a ruler. And exactly what we cannot detect in this way is his real being. This is even true for modern science. What we use to call "matter," what we describe as dead objects that we may define once for all, is actually a world of happenings, of movements and events. Even the essence of any so-called dead object is indeed "existence," life, a world of changing positions or radiations to all directions and we possess no adequate words to describe it. How much more will this be true with regard to God. If the very being, the "essence" of God is his living "existence," his life itself, this has far-reaching consequences.

Since we cannot find God except in his life, his acts, his manifestations, we have to concentrate on Jesus Christ. Catholic scholars like *Edward Schillebeeckx,* born 1914 in Belgium, professor in Louvain, Belgium, 1956, and one year later in Nimwegen, Netherlands, point to Jesus' whole ministry with its openness to all human wants and deeds, sufferings and joys, estrangement from and longing for God. For Schillebeeckx the Christ-event goes on in the experiences of the church. There was an experience of God in Jesus' life and death which repeats itself time and again in the church, always interpreted anew according to different cultural backgrounds. Thus there is no one official interpretation, but there are continuously new ones of the same experience of God.[21] Protestant theologians like *Jürgen Moltmann* and especially *Eberhard Jüngel,* born 1935, professor in East Berlin in 1961, Zurich in 1966, and Tübingen since 1969, focus their view on the cross of Jesus. For Moltmann God is the suffering God, the great companion and fellow-sufferer who understands humanity. If God were not able to suffer, he could not be able to love. At the same time, he is not a powerless sufferer but the one who acts in resurrecting Jesus and by this opens a new dimension of history, a history of love and liberation, which goes on in the lives of his believers.[22] Jüngel takes the identification of God's being with his existence in his acts so seriously that he speaks with Luther of the death of God on the cross. Such a statement is only possible, without becoming sacrilegious, when one realizes that, in this instance, death is not an end but the overcoming of finiteness. The human nature of Jesus is not a secondary attribute to a God who in himself would not be human. God is the background "mystery" of all human and earthly existence; he is "God as mystery of the world" (as the title of his last work runs). Love is not a quality of God, one among others. God *is* love, the love which happens, concentrated in one focus, in the death of Jesus on the cross. Jesus is the event of love which draws humanity into itself so that we also do not only "have" love, but *are* loving in the whole of our existence and become loving always anew.[23]

Having followed Schillebeeckx, Moltmann, and Jüngel up to this point, we must stop and ask: Are we not back again either to an understanding of Jesus as teacher and example in the case of Schillebeeckx, or to a deification of human love in its corporate, social form in the case of Moltmann, or in its more individual form in the case of Jüngel? At this point we have to go back to the interest of patristic theology in an immanent trinity. Jüngel himself emphasizes in his earlier book *Gottes Sein ist im Werden*[24] that the church always declared that God is Father, Son, and Spirit from eternity to eternity, before and after there was an earth. This means, according to Jüngel, that God is never an object closed in itself and therefore unchangeable, dead; God is life, the living love. What is unchangeable is his faithfulness which we shall encounter time and again. When we say that God is a person, one person, this is an adequate image, since God is certainly one God with no other gods beside him. But can we think of a person without somebody or at least something outside of it? A person has eyes to see, ears to hear, hands to touch. But if God is really one, there cannot be any other person or even any other being or object on which he would depend. Therefore the church said that God is three persons. Again, this is an image—inadequate perhaps with respect to the oneness of God, but very adequate with respect to the living quality of God. The life of God's love streams from the Father to the Son and back from the Son to the Father; at the same time it radiates and creates as the Spirit. Just as the love between father and mother creates the possibility of life for a baby so that it could literally not live without the sphere of that love, so the life of love in God himself creates the world and its beings. And since we cannot conceive of an abstract being of God, we have to say that he *is* this life of love from eternity to eternity, remaining one and the same love and yet expressing itself in a living and infinitely changing spectrum of possible manifestations. Thus the doctrine of trinity does not define God. On the contrary, it keeps his mystery. It says that his oneness is to be taken so seriously that his life is to be seen as life in himself, being lived between Father and Son, even before it creates, in the radiation of the Spirit, a world loved by God. While the idea of three persons is an image, all of our words about God—even about nature, as modern science has shown—are but images. This image is adequate and excellent just because it shows clearly its character as an image, pointing to the truth, but not falsely suggesting that it could captivate truth in a mathematical definition.

Where do we go from here? If God is life, even event, can we pray to an event?[25] If he lives in the world as the power of love, as manifested in Jesus' death and resurrection, how can we see him as the one over against us, speaking to us, challenging us, comforting us, damning us and reconciling us? There is one thing I am sure of, namely that I cannot offer any easy solution. What I suggest is that you listen attentively to Luke, because I think that he contributes some thoughts which have not been taken seriously enough; nor have they been applied to our modern problems.

III.
History and Salvation History—
What Do They Mean Today?

1. What is history?

There is a story about a Texan tourist, visiting his friend in Zurich and seeing, for the first time, the chain of the snow-covered Alps soaring into the blue sky beyond the blue lake on an incredibly clear autumn day. "Well," he said, "we do not have Alps like those, but if we had them, they would be much higher." It is one of the contingencies of history that he has been born in a vast and rather flat country, whereas his friend has been born in a very small country with high mountains. This contingency has shaped the Texan, who is used to thinking on a big scale, and also the Swiss, who is proud of showing the beauty of Swiss mountains to foreign tourists. It is exactly this contingency that the modern analytical philosophy of history stresses.

What is history? The term "history" means, first, the facts themselves which have happened in the past, the so-called historical facts. However, even if we use the word in this sense, we presuppose that these facts have happened in a correlation and consequence. This leads to the other meaning of the word. "History" also means our knowledge of these facts and our understanding which puts them into a pattern of causes and effects, actions and reactions, etc. There are five points which seem to be essential for the modern concept of history:[26]

(1) On the one hand, the past has happened without us; it is given to us in an objective, unchangeable way. The past shapes us, the Texan or the Swiss; we cannot shape the past.

(2) On the other hand, it is only a later generation that understands the past, because they know of what has come out of these historical facts. Each event has its future, and it is only the historian of a later period who knows the future which has come into being since a particular event happened. The attack on the British tea ship in the port of Boston in 1773 is a fact. But in that year

nobody knew what it was. Was it a hazardous enterprise which would lead to hard punishment? Was it the outbreak of juvenile wantonness or of a suffering population? However one would have judged then, only few could not have known what it really was. Most people could not have said: "This is the beginning of the War of Independence." The historian can say so, and only the historian knows what really happened there. But the historian cannot say it in an unbiased way. He or she may say "the beginning of independence" or "the mutiny of the Bostonians, the first clear manifestation of secession." It is impossible to write history in an impartial way. Even the selection of facts itself, before any interpretation is added, is always act of partiality. The facts that an idealistic historian considers important are different from those that a Marxist selects. Even the experience of what happens by a contemporary is by necessity partial because different people experience the same events in quite different ways.

(3) What about this future of an event that a historian sees? Can the historian compare hundreds and thousands of historical developments and abstract from them some pattern, some laws of a developing history? Hegel thought so; he assumed he was able to detect a divine spirit unfolding in the course of history. Marx also thought so; but he detected the hard rules of economic conditions and their respective consequences. But can we use at all the pattern of cause and effect, as used in natural science? We can say that the event in Boston caused other events which finally led to the way and to American independence. And yet, should we not speak of "entailing" these events, rather than "causing" them, because what really happened was but one possible consequence of many? The uproar could also have died down without any change of the situation. Or it could have led to British punishment which the town of Boston would have suffered without resistance. Or a hundred other developments could have happened. Again, the contingency of history is obvious. That it happened the way we know was dependent on hundreds of contingent facts, on the kind of people who were involved, on the choice of words by a speaker who summoned the population to resistance, on the date on which the first attack took place, on the situation in the neighboring towns and countries, etc.

(4) Are we standing over against history so that history teaches us to understand our own existence, as an existentialist historian would perhaps see it? Is history, as a Greek of the first century B.C. defines it, "philosophy teaching by example"?[27] Would we, just by understanding history, even be able to master it by our decisions and actions, as an activist would see it? It is certainly true that history can teach us and give us new insights and thus lead us to specific decisions and actions. It is also true that we by our decisions and following actions can make history. And yet, this is only part of the truth. It is equally true that history decides on us and forms us. If a man or a woman is born a slave, he or she may know nothing of history, and even if he or she does so, the consequences he or she will draw from this knowledge in thoughts and actions will be quite different from those of the master, even contrary to them. It may even be some gesture of love or some shock that we have experienced as an infant which becomes decisive for our mode of action thirty years later. And then, it may be a storm which destroys our ships, an earthquake which shakes the walls of our enemies so that we meet our defeat or gain our victory. Is not the other Greek right who declared, three centuries later, that "history is an unmethodical matter" (*amethodos hule*)?[28] No doubt, contingency in manifold forms is an equally important factor in a person's own insights, decisions, and actions. Thus modern philosophy speaks of the person as the "reference-subject" of history, a subject that stands in manifold ways, actively and passively, in reference to history.

(5) This gives to the historically single, special, and individual event or situation or person an eminent importance. Just what cannot be detected logically from the past nor be calculated for the future, are the most important items in history. Therefore, a historical event is, first of all, a single, special and individual event. We can say: "The attack on the British tea ship in Boston *was* the beginning of American independence." We cannot change this sentence into a sentence with no reference to a specific time and situation. That means, it would be nonsense to declare: "An attack on a tea ship *is* the beginning of independence." This leads to two conclusions which become enormously important for theological think-

ing. First, a historical event cannot simply be taken over into our time. We cannot re-present it in such a way that it becomes as such alive today. Its importance for today lies exactly in its being past. The action of the Bostonians is still relevant because Americans are still living independently because of its having happened at that time. But it would not have any relevance if we repeated it in the 1980s. This is totally different from actions based on laws of nature. The act of the first person who heated water until it boiled can be repeated in the same way thousands of years later. Neither can we realize the importance of a historical fact by putting ourselves back to that year in order to repeat the existential experience of those Bostonians, because the importance of their action lay in its future consequences of which they knew nothing in their time. Maybe they are simply afraid of or totally indifferent to it. Hence, any timeless understanding of history which would dispense with the contingent factors of its time would blind us against the special character of all historical events, which is exactly the most important factor in them.

2. The New Testament as history

What is the relevance of all this for the understanding of New Testament history? The problem is obvious. The New Testament declares that a relative historical event, the crucifixion of Jesus around 30 A.D., which was dependent on many contingencies, is the absolute revelation of God. It also declares that this event is relevant for people of today in a direct way, not merely so that it had some consequences in history which entailed other consequences whose chain has not yet been broken. How shall we understand this?

Two extreme positions have been defended. The first understands God as revealing himself in the totality of history, be it the history of Israel (and the church) or universal history. This is, as we have seen, the thesis of Hegel and his followers. The second understands the Christ-event as the eschatological event and even as the end of history because, whatever the historical changes may be, the meaning of this event remains the same for people of all generations and all countries, either because in it a ransom has been paid for all people, as normal orthodoxy would put it, or because in it the meaning of human existence has been revealed for all people, as an existential theology would put it.[29]

The problem of the first solution is that the cross of Jesus Christ becomes one historical event among others, though the central or most important one. If so, its meaning for today, if understood historically, is mediated through various and contingent developments of history so that it becomes clear where history is clearly connected with the events in Palestine, for instance, in European history, but is hidden for those of another history, for instance Asians, unless they accept European history as their own. The problem of the second solution is that history becomes meaningless. People accept the truth of orthodox belief in the redemptory power of the cross or of its existential model enlightening them, apart from history. They are directly related to the event of 30 A.D., and only in a secondary way they may be driven to get engaged in the history of their time (or also to withdraw from this history) and to learn something from past history.

When we now turn to Luke and check his approach over against the five points in our brief survey on modern philosophy of history, we find quite a measure of agreement with them. This, of course, says nothing about the meaning of the history of Jesus Christ, about the truth or untruth of the gospel. It says simply that Luke understood the Christ-event as history and that he did not exclude the contingencies of history. Later we shall have to ask in what way this history is for him more important than any other history.

3. First point: God's act outside us

One often reproaches Luke with his understanding of himself as a historian. He says so in the preface to the Gospel, and it looks as if the mere fact of a safe tradition of the historical events of life and death of Jesus Christ would be the guarantee of faith: "... that you may know the truth concerning the things of which you have been informed" (1:4). The first word of the adult Jesus which we read in Luke's Gospel is "today," and this "today" of the fulfilled prophecy is a historical day on which Jesus preached in

Nazareth (4:21). *Hans Conzelmann* has put this in sharp contrast to Paul's interpretation of a prophetic promise: "Behold, now is the acceptable time" (2 Cor. 6:2), where the "now" describes the time of the proclamation of the gospel, which goes on up to today.[30] We shall ask later whether there is really such a contrast between Paul and Luke. At the moment, it may suffice to see that Luke is well aware of the fact that the saving event lies outside of humanity, *extra nos,* as the Reformers used to emphasize. It is not a movement of the human heart or soul or mind which saves a person; it is God's action. And God is no part of the person; his decisive act is, locally and temporally, outside the hearer of the gospel. It took place in the Palestine of the first thirty years of our era, in the history of a life and death on this earth. But when Paul declares that the basis of the faith of the Corinthians had been taught them by himself to whom it also had been handed down, it is also a report of some events in history which reached them by a careful tradition: namely that Christ died, was buried, has been raised from the dead, and was seen by Cephas and the twelve (1 Cor. 15:3–5). Paul does not include the earthly ministry of Jesus, and we shall discuss this point in the next lecture. Nonetheless, it is a sequence of events within the history of Palestine within the year of, probably, 30 A.D.; it is a nucleus of *heilsgeschichte.* Luke expands this history, on the one hand, back to Israel, on the other, into the history of the church. Again, is this essentially different from what Paul does, when he emphasizes, on the one hand, with his tradition, that this happened "according to the Scriptures," and, on the other, that the risen Christ appeared later to the five hundred, to James and to all the apostles, finally to Paul himself, and that all of them preached, since then, the same message? We shall discuss the differences in the understanding of these points in the next chapter. Nonetheless, there is, also with Paul, a kind of *heilsgeschichte* which leads from Israel to Jesus Christ and from him into the church.

Luke is certainly not the inventor of *heilsgeschichte.* There is some hint of it in the pre-Pauline tradition, and it is even clearer in the pre-Markan one; it is also evident in the beginning of the collection of Jesus' sayings which is common to Matthew and Luke. Mark reports the parable of the vineyard tenants. It describes the proprietor who creates the vineyard and sends his servants to their destiny. Thus the parable tells about God electing Israel and delegating the prophets and about Israel rejecting them. The end of the parable opens up to the present time of decision and to the future history; the lord will farm out his land to other tenants; God will grant salvation to other people. Again, there is a *heilsgeschichte* which goes from the beginning of Israel, described in biblical terms, to the post-Easter history of the church (Mark 12:1–11). This is certainly true for Mark, but even if the parable went back to Jesus himself, its end would point to the future after the time of his definite rejection by his people. In the layer common to Matthew and Luke, there is the word about all the prophets, sent by God's wisdom and rejected by Israel, until all the righteous blood shed on earth will come over God's people now in Jesus' time.

In all this the first Christians simply followed Old Testament patterns. In the Yahwist's story in Genesis, after a continuous decline God elects Abraham and starts a new history. This will lead to all nations being blessed (or, maybe, blessing themselves) in Abraham's name. The scheme of Deuteronomy tells the story of the alternating actions and reactions of God's and Israel's deeds; the book of Wisdom, according to which God's wisdom acts in all the human actors and even in the natural phenomena of the history from Adam to the entry into the land of promise (Wisd. 10–12). What the New Testament continued was the Old Testament emphasis on God standing as the Lord of history, over against humanity, electing humanity, saving humanity by his own divine acts in history. As God created people, before they could reflect upon it and believe it, so he saved them, before they even knew of it, *extra hominem*, outside of humanity.

4. Second point: The partiality of the historian

The second point reminded us that history as told by people is necessarily partial. Even the selection of facts to be told or to be left out is in itself a partial decision. There is no doubt that Luke knows that. The sign of the manger, mentioned three times in the Christmas story, means nothing in itself. The manger was a normal cradle for all except wealthy homes. It needed the proclamation of the angels and the testimony of the shepherds to be understandable. The crucifixion of Jesus was not understood by its eyewitnesses, let alone by the twelve who had fled. Without the interpretation of the risen Lord and its later continuation by the apostles, it would not have meant anything to those who knew or heard about it. Therefore, Luke points time and again to the Scriptures that only can show what really happened.

But there is even more in it. It is a caricature of Luke when one maintains that, for Luke, the guarantee of the fact by an eyewitness would be the basis of faith. It is, in the preface, the testimony of the "eyewitnesses and ministers of the word." According to Acts 1:21–22 "the men who have accompanied us during all the time that the Lord Jesus went in and out among us" must become, by God's special act, also "witnesses to Jesus' resurrection." This is stressed by the distinction between the believers in general (most of whom would have been eyewitnesses at least of the final stage of the ministry of Jesus) who "spoke the word of God," and the apostles who "gave their testimony to the resurrection of the Lord Jesus" (Acts 4:31, 33). And what about the famous "today" in Jesus' sermon in Nazareth? Of course, it means the day of his preaching there. But it says that "today this Scripture has been fulfilled in your hearing" (literally: in your ears). "In your ears" sounds like the existentialist "in your self-understanding." Also according to Luke, it is in the hearing of the message that the salvation of God becomes true, and Luke knows that the fact of Jesus' preaching itself is totally ambiguous. One can understand it as a bold manifestation of superciliousness, as a crazy vision of a dreamer, as the truth of God or as many other things. Its interpretation as the fulfillment of the Scriptures is a very partial one indeed.

The same "today" is repeated in the story of the publican Zacchaeus: "Today salvation has come to this house" (19:9). Again, this is the historical day of Jesus' visit to his house, but it follows immediately after the publican's decision to give away half of his goods. The sentence is awkward in the context of the story, because Jesus' saying is now addressed to Zacchaeus, but speaks of him in the third person ("since he is also a son of Abraham"). Many exegetes think that it is only Luke who has inserted this promise of

Zacchaeus. Personally, I think that it has been added in a pre-Lukan stage, but if it was done by Luke himself, it would even more emphasize his understanding. Thus again, the "today" is the day on which people understand the historical event of Jesus' coming as something which concerns them and alters their lives. In a story peculiar to Luke (17:19), "your faith has saved you" is said to one of the ten healed lepers who came back to thank God and to adore Jesus. "Salvation" (the same Greek word as "healing") has come to all of them, but has been understood only by one.

This becomes even clearer in Acts. True, in Antioch Paul speaks of "the word of this salvation" which "was sent to us" (in contrast to the contemporary Jews in Jerusalem), not of salvation itself (13:26). In 3:16, however, it is the "name" of Jesus, that means the preached Jesus, which made the cripple strong, and in 4:12 salvation comes through the name of Jesus or through Jesus himself, both expressions being equivalent. Jesus himself is present in the proclamation of his name, in the authoritative preaching. Jesus' passion, resurrection, and proclamation form one event or at least one homogeneous period of events in Luke 24:46–47 as well as in Acts 17:3; 5:30–32; 10:41–42; 13:31. According to Acts 26:23 it is Jesus who, after having suffered and risen, proclaims himself to Israel and the nations. This shows that the formula of the first verse of Luke's Gospel is to be taken seriously. Luke's narrative concerns the events that have found their "fulness . . . among us," meaning in the church of those to whom they have proclaimed.[31] Again, we have to probe into deeper layers in the next chapter in order to see how the events and their proclamation belong together and are distinguished by Paul on the one and Luke on the other hand.

5. Third point: The future of an event as one of many possibilities

World history is not a clear sequence of causes and effects. The future of an event is not fixed in advance; there are various possible results of the same historical event. Even if what actually happens is caused by a former event, it is only one of several possibilities. Therefore the course of world history cannot be predicted in the way a course of a natural process can be foreseen. The difference is not absolute, as a modern scientist knows, but in our experience it is very clear. If I throw a stone into a lake, I can predict that it will sink. If I throw a stone into the king's palace, I cannot predict whether it causes a revolution and perhaps the end of the monarchy, or my imprisonment without any other effects, or nothing at all because it passes unnoticed. Even when looking back one can say: "The throwing of that stone was the signal that caused the running together of the citizens; this sudden manifestation of their majority and power caused the attack on the palace which caused the death of the king, etc." One has always to admit that it could have gone quite differently and that many contingencies led to the final result. We are not even sure whether it was really that throwing of the stone which set the people into motion. Perhaps they made their assault just by chance at the same time. If we understand by *heilsgeschichte* a sequence of historical events that are fixed from the beginning to its goal by God's decision and plan, it is Matthew or even Paul and not Luke who invented the New Testament *heilsgeschichte.*

According to the first paragraph of the first Gospel, the history runs from Abraham to Jesus after a prefixed plan of God in exactly three times fourteen generations. In the parallel passage of Luke 3:23–38 there is also a family tree leading from Jesus back to Adam. There are actually eleven units of seven generations so that Jesus starts the twelfth unit. This goes back to the apocalyptic idea of an eon of twelve "weeks," the last of which is the messianic time as an ultimate period before the definite end and the coming of the kingdom of God. There is even a repetition of some names to be found, because without them the calculation of eleven times seven would not work. But Luke knows nothing about this background or, if he knows, he does not even give a hint to such understanding. In his presentation, it is a motley and contingent pattern of known and unknown human beings. At any point of the line God could have chosen another son and, especially, he could have sent Jesus earlier or later without changing anything in a prefixed numerical pattern. Paul, writing Romans 9–11, declares that the Jews had to reject Jesus so that the Gentiles would come to the faith and that those in their turn would make Israel jealous so that it also would convert as a whole (11:11–26).

Luke knows nothing of this. He knows, of course, the fact of the mission to the Gentiles and of their favorable response, but he sees it in a very pragmatic way. The Lord invited first the poor ones in the city, the Jews, and then there were still places free in the dining hall, so he invited also those from the country, the Gentiles (14:21–23, a passage peculiar to Luke). Luke also transposes the saying about the first becoming the last to the end of the short simile of the door closed to latecomers (13:30). In his interpretation, these are the Palestinian Jews in whose marketplaces Jesus has taught, whereas people from the four quarters of the heaven will sit in the bosom of Abraham. But again, he changes the wording. He says: "There are last who will be first, and there are first who will be last." There is no *heilsgeschichtlich* law; *some* Gentiles will be first and *some* Jews will be last, but not heathendom as such or Israel as such. This also fits into the pattern of Acts. There are 3,000, then 5,000, then even more, finally ten thousands of Jerusalemite Jews that accept the gospel, and there are also Gentiles that persecute Paul. There are believers and non-believers in both groups. True, there is a prerogative of Israel. As Jesus taught in its marketplaces, so the apostles preach first to Israel and only after being heard by some and rejected by others do they go to the Gentiles.

It is true that Luke speaks of the providence, the plan, and the will of God, according to which something happens. He loves verbs with the prefix "pro-" indicating that something has been thought, planned, proclaimed before it happened. He uses a Greek phrase when he lets Jesus say to Paul: "It hurts you [or: it will be hard to you] to kick against the goads" (Acts 26:14). It is true that Luke is not so much an apocalypticist as a preacher of God's providence in the private lives of the believers and in some crucial periods of the church. He is also interested in miracles of the apostles, in dreams and visions and angel messages, by which God gives some guidance to his church. But just that shows that this is not actually *heilsgeschichte*; it is rather an individual divine guidance. Therefore the conversion of the individual or of a whole group is important, as is the prayer for such guidance.

This providence of God does not cover the course of Old Testament history as such. Paul in his sermon at Antioch seems, according to Luke, to start an account of Israel's history, but he stops short when coming to David and jumps from there directly to Jesus Christ, announced by John the Baptist—similarly as the genuine Paul of the letters sees a direct connection from Abraham to Jesus—and it is only now that a verb with the prefix "pro-" appears. Neither the conjunction nor the preposition "before" is used in the Old Testament part. David or the prophets know and may even speak about the coming of Christ, but there is no *heilsgeschichte* leading up to him.

This accounts for an astonishing fact. Luke 1–2 shows a certain motion. The chapters start in a family righteous and pious according to the law of Moses and lead to the coming of Jesus. The story of the announcement of the birth of John is almost repeated, but at the same time it is also surpassed by that of the announcement to Mary, and the same parallels of repetition and surpassing come again in the respective stories of the birth and name-giving of the two and in the following hymns of praise. There is a theologically new hold on history. It is not merely the fact that John is, in 1:16–17, clearly described as the forerunner of God, as the Old Testament quotation says it, but is boldly interpreted as the forerunner of Jesus Christ. This is not so different from what Paul and the other evangelists do, though more outspoken in the direct sequence of the two verses. Much more important is the astounding choice of a story of a contemporary family as a vehicle for the events of Jesus' coming. This is not history of centuries ago, which has already become Holy Scripture. It is history of people, perhaps still personally known to some readers. The prophets who speak of Jesus' coming fate are not texts but living persons, older contemporaries of both John and Jesus. God has, according to Luke, chosen, in a contingent way, an elderly priest and his wife to introduce the story of his son. Again, we have to ask in the next chapter what it means that Luke does not present a *heilsgeschichtlich* concept but does speak of God's plan and providence with respect to people living with Jesus or shortly before or in his church.

6. Fourth point: History made by man?

The fourth note of history, as seen in modern philosophy,

is the insight that it is not shaped exclusively or even primarily by people. The person is subject of reference. Again, this is what Luke underlines often. Augustus introduces a new tax in his empire, but he has no idea as to what he is really doing (Luke 2:1–7). The Roman officer Felix makes a decision to keep Paul in custody in order to get some bribe, but he has no idea as to what he is really doing (Acts 24:26). The emperor brings the parents of Jesus to Bethlehem and is in this way the cause of his birth in the town of promise. His employee is the cause of bringing Paul and his message to the capital of the empire. Neither knew what he had done, and neither wanted to do it. Thus the real subject is God. And yet Luke certainly does not say that the adoption of a higher state tax or the openness to bribery was God's will. What he says is much simpler. He says that God can use totally profane events like the adoption of a new tax or even amoral decisions of people to proffer his history. He understands this in a rather pragmatic way. He does not assume that all history is a direct outflow of God's will, but he is convinced that God can use all history to bring forth what he wills, whenever and wherever it pleases him.

Undoubtedly, God also uses the conscious will and work of persons who want to be obedient to him, and this is the usual way in which the gospel is preached. But it is never so that people could, in some way, find God out and become aware of his tricks in order to understand beforehand why this or that must happen in order to effect this or that. Although, in Luke's Gospel, the disciples recognize Jesus as the Messiah, the mystery of his suffering (not of his messiahship as in Mark) is hidden from them until the risen Christ explains it to them. The same is true, after Easter, with respect to the mission to the Gentiles. It had been ordered by the risen Lord already in Acts 1:8, but up to the death of Stephen and even beyond it the twelve just stayed in Jerusalem. The persecution of the Jerusalem church in that time showed the face of a very serious defeat of the cause of the gospel. No Christian would have wished it or could have understood it as a victory. It was only much later that the church realized that this mishap actually brought the gospel to the Gentiles. Even then, God's government was not clearly visible. There was quite an action of God with miracles, dreams, and angels urging Peter, against all his doubts and hesitance, finally to preach the gospel to the heathen officer Cornelius (Acts 8:4–5; 10:1–11, 18). And yet, in some way, this whole action died down, and the really important mission to the Gentiles was started by the refugees of the persecution who, very hesitantly, without clear signs of God, and only partially, began to preach Christ not only to Jews but also to Gentiles of the same town. This happened especially in Antioch, which became, not much later, the center of Paul's activity and the base for his decisive missionary journeys (11:19–20, 25; 13:2). What is it about this togetherness of God's and humanity's acts? We have to take this question up in the next chapter.

7. Fifth point: What about dogmatic statements?

The final point of analytical philosophy of history is the impossibility of changing a historical statement into a "dogmatic" statement neutral as to time and place. If we take this seriously, the old problem rises again: How can we proclaim the relative events of a relative history as the absolute truth? If we say: "Jesus has died in Jerusalem in about 30 A.D. because of his rejection by humanity, and, in his intention, for the sake of humankind," can we change this into a sentence, not related to time and place: "The death of Jesus is the reconciliation of all sins," even if the name Jesus still refers to a particular man in history? This is the problem of the third chapter: In what way is the Christ-event, located within the Roman Empire, dated within the first century A.D., the *absolute*—we may also say the *eschatological*—event of God?

IV.
The Crucified and Risen Christ—
How Is He Present Today?

There are not only stories about Texans; there are also stories about the Swiss. I have heard that when God had just created the world he found a Swiss already there and asked him whether he was pleased with the world. He answered: "Well, what is all that without mountains?" So God created the Alps. But the Swiss was not yet satisfied; he needed cows too, and God created a herd of cows. Now, the Swiss went immediately to milk them. God asked him whether he now had all that he wanted and tasted some of the milk. "One twenty, please, for the milk," said the Swiss. This story has its depth. As long as God was creating the world, the mountains, and the cows, he was recognizable as God. But when God simply encounters us in an everyday event, in the drinking of a glass of milk for instance, how is he to be distinguished from a normal tourist? This is exactly the problem with which we have to wrestle today because God did come into our world to drink his glass of milk, though not with Swiss but with Galilean farmers. How can we speak of this event, relative to time and place, part of a contingent history, as the absolute event, relevant to people of all times and places?

1. First solution: *Heilsgeschichte*

Luke tells stories, a varied wealth of stories, held together by the fact that they all are related to Jesus of Nazareth. This is his decisive contribution to the New Testament. Telling stories about a man living and dying in a specific time and place, with the claim to write a Gospel, expresses the belief that salvation happened. Therefore God is to be found within this world and its history, and yet clearly outside of ourselves, in a time and a place different from our time and place. Such a statement is merely a paraphrase of the problem. How shall we understand that God is to be found in the world, though not part of the world? And how shall we understand that he is to be found in another time and place than the time and place in which we are living, though being directly relevant to us?

The first solution would be the pattern of *heilsgeschichte*. This would mean that an initial event, understood as a miracle granted by God, had its historical effects which are still relevant. The miracle of the escape of Israel through the Red Sea was the beginning of its journey through the desert which led it to the land of promise, to which it came back, first after the Babylonian captivity, and after centuries of exile recently again. In the same way the victory in the way of independence is still relevant for the existence of the United States. Whether one sees the process under the continuous guidance of God or rather as a natural course of history initiated by the miraculous help of God as its first cause, it is, at any rate, this process which connects us with God's initial act. There is some truth in this solution. The miracle of Pentecost is, in the book of Acts, certainly a miracle of God which initiated a history of mission. Since God is God of humanity, he acts in history, because people are always part of history. When God uses humans, he acts within the human world and its rules of cause and effect. When God comforts Paul in a dream, this is the cause of his staying in Corinth, and this again is the cause of the formation of a large church there (Acts 18:9–11). And yet, this is, as we have seen, not the solution of Luke. The importance of the Christ-event is not simply that of a first cause which started a historical process. In the proclamation of the apostles it comes directly to the hearers, not mediated by a long development in which, by and large, the first beginning slowly disappears in a more and more distant past. Even without the war of the 1770s the United States would no longer be a British colony; thus that beginning is no longer of first importance. Nor does Luke give us a pattern of God's continuous *heilsgeschichtlich* guidance so that we could see some definite rules of God's acting in history. The God of Israel is certainly the same as the Father of Jesus, the God of the church in Jerusalem the same as the God of that in Rome. And yet there is no possibility of "New Testament Abstracts," of abstracting a pattern which repeats itself and, therefore, allows one to predict a future development. The church of Rome is different from that of Jerusalem; what was right for that one is not good for this one. And this is not a logical progress or decline but a consequence of surprising new initiatives of God, which traveled on unexpected new roads into unexpected new territories.

If God were nothing more than a miraculous first cause which led to a historical development without him, he would not be God in and for the world. Also, if he were nothing more than a fixed and intelligible pattern or law ruling all historical development, he would no longer be God, but just part of the world.

2. Second solution: Orthodoxy

Should we adhere to the second solution and simply believe on the basis of an incomprehending trust in the authority of the apostolic proclamation of the Christ-event as being our salvation? Again, there is some truth in it. God's presence cannot be proved and demonstrated but can only be proclaimed and experienced. It is the risen Lord who gives his disciples the interpretation of what has happened in his passion and resurrection; he also explains the Scriptures. Then, it is the apostles who proclaim the truth of his resurrection, and they alone are witnesses to it. To be sure, we need dogmatic statements, even honorable liturgical formulae that we do not understand. But they are not the truth. They are like barriers along the turnpike. They stop us driving into the swamp on the right or into the canyon on the left. They may guard us against dangers which we do not see or which will appear only later on—and therefore we do not yet understand what they mean. They may with their cat's eyes even show us the direction in which we have to drive, but they are not the road which brings us to our goal; if we confounded the rails with the road, catastrophe would be unavoidable.

Therefore this approach, again, is not the solution of Luke. His Christology is far from being clear. According to his Gospel, the crowds call Jesus a prophet (7:16); the disciples of Emmaus do the same (24:19); and Luke, in a saying specifically ascribed to him, lets even Jesus speak of himself in this category (13:33: "It cannot be that a prophet should perish away from Jerusalem"). Peter and Stephen in Acts 3:22–23 and 7:37 proclaim Jesus as *the* prophet like Moses. He is also savior (Luke 2:11; Acts 5:31; 13:23) or leader

(Acts 3:15; 5:31). When Luke speaks of Jesus being the servant of God, we do not know whether he thinks of the suffering servant of Isaiah (as in Acts 3:13–26) or of the promised Davidic king (as in Acts 4:25–30). In a number of passages he introduces the title "Lord" when speaking of the earthly Jesus, but in Acts 2:36 he says that God made him Lord in his resurrection and ascension.

Even more chaotic is his usage of the term "Son of God." Luke 1:35 declares that Jesus is the Son of God, because he is born from the Virgin Mary upon whom the Spirit of God came. But the family tree explains that Jesus is supposedly son of Joseph, son of Heli, etc., so that he is indirectly son of Adam who is the son of God (3:23–38). Just before that passage, God's heavenly voice declared him his son after the baptism in the Jordan. Without doubt, Acts 13:33 sees the fulfillment of this verse (Ps. 2:7) and therefore the date on which his divine sonship started, not in Jesus' baptism, but in his resurrection. Luke lets Peter speak of "Jesus of Nazareth, a man attested to you by God with mighty works and wonders and signs," whom God "has made Lord and Christ" in the resurrection (Acts 2:22, 36), or Paul of a "man" whom God has appointed as judge in the last judgment (Acts 17:31). When Jesus confesses before the high priest to be the "Son of man," this is—and Luke alters here the Markan report—understood as equivalent to "Son of God" (22:67–70). This is all but clear. Is Jesus a man working some miracles, a prophet, *the* prophet, the Son of man, the suffering or the kingly Servant of God, the Son of God through his miraculous birth, through his descent from Adam, through divine designation during his baptism or through the event of his resurrection? It is obvious that Luke does not think that any title is sufficient to describe the truth fully. Human language possesses no term to catch the mystery of who Jesus is. Therefore the mere act of accepting an official Christology, handed down by apostolic or biblical or ecclesiastical authority, will never bring humanity into a decisive relationship with him.

When we come to Luke's soteriological formulae we detect something very similar. He is not opposed to a soteriology in which human salvation is rooted in the death of Jesus. Once, in Acts 20:28, he takes up a phrase which reminds the reader of Psalm

74(73):2 ("the congregation which thou hast bought off [or: ransomed] to the tribe of thy heritage") and of the understanding of salvation in Revelation 5:9 ("thou [the lamb] didst ransom by thy blood men for God from every tribe and people and nation and hast made them a kingdom and priests to our God"). He quotes this phrase as if it were some foreign language, actually writing: "the church of *God* which he obtained with his own blood." He probably did not realize that he used the phrase in a context in which it speaks of the blood of God, not of Christ. Similarly, most Germans pray "*Vater user*," which is nonsense, exactly as "Father our" would be, simply because the Latin address "Pater noster" has been taken over without much thought about its meaning. Whether Luke wrote the words of the institution of the chalice is not certain, because it is missing in some ancient manuscripts. If he did so, as I personally think, it is again a case of more or less mechanic repetition of a liturgy; for the phrase of the liturgy used in the Pauline churches, "This cup is the new covenant in my blood," is combined with the last part of a totally different liturgical phrase which he found in Mark: "This is my blood shed for you." Here "blood" stands in the nominative, not in the dative. This is an extremely awkward sentence, much more awkward than in an English translation like, "This cup is the new covenant in my blood, the one shed for you." More important is the omission of Mark 10:45: "The Son of man also came not to be served but to serve, and to give his life as a ransom for many." It is true that the whole Markan passage has been left out by Luke, perhaps for other reasons than avoiding a doctrinal statement about an expiatory sacrifice. But he replaces this crucial saying by two other words, of which we shall speak presently, Luke 19:10 and 22:27, where nothing is said about an atoning or ransoming death of Christ. In the sermon of Paul on the Areopagus, Jesus' death is not even mentioned, only his resurrection and his final coming as judge (Acts 17:31). In the sermons of Peter and Paul to the Jews, the crucifixion of Jesus is merely used as proof of their guilt, and it is the resurrection which is the saving event.

Thus Luke offers no dogmatic formula that a believer simply would have to accept as truth in order to be saved. Such formulae might secure the non-worldliness of God, his alienness, his incomprehensible divinity. If God became simply the content of a formula he would not really have come into our world; he would remain something like a ghost to whom we have no relation. Humans would think that they had mastered God if God accepted the formula; but this would be an illusion, because in this case God would remain a total stranger; inhuman, not because he is to be distinguished from humans, as the creator from his creature, but because he has only entered the brain of humans, not their world. And for those who would not accept the formula on mere trust in the authority of the church, the God of the formula would mean nothing at all.

3. Third solution: Existential interpretation

A third possible solution comes closer to Luke's understanding. Is the story of Jesus Christ still relevant because it shows what human existence in all times and in all places and what God's unchangeable meaning for human existence is? There is quite a bit of truth in this approach. Humans of all times and places are beings who experience their limits and the fear of reaching them, but also unexpected help and the joy which is caused by this, beings who know about life and death and who reflect upon themselves, who have some unquenchable desire to go beyond themselves and can decide for or against loving the neighbor. In all this humans are distinguished from the animal. Jesus' sayings or deeds, even the totality of his way of living and dying, may certainly teach one much about oneself and one's possibilities to live and to die. Luke knows about that. Is he not interested very much in the conversion of individuals? Does he not tell stories of conversions as teaching examples for people of all times and all places? Does not the publican stand for all the outsiders of the world? And yet, these stories are so varied. The rich ruler has to sell all that he possesses (18:22); the chief tax collector is praised for giving up half of his goods (19:8). One who wants to follow Jesus is not even permitted to say farewell to his family (9:61–62); another one is not allowed to follow Jesus, but sent back to his family (8:38–39). Unlike Mark, Luke distinguishes sometimes between demands of Jesus addressed to his disciples and demands on all believers.[32] He also distinguishes clearly the different periods of the church. The life of the first congregation in Jerusalem is not the pattern to be followed by the churches in Asia Minor or in Greece. He knows about the historically unique situation of the first years. The decision of the apostles' council not to put the "yoke [of the Mosaic law] upon the neck of the disciples which neither our fathers nor we have been able to bear" (Acts 15:10) is not valid for the Jewish Christians in Jerusalem, who "are all zealous for the law," nor for Paul himself, who is "to live in observance of the law" when visiting them (21:20–24).

Again, it is a motley picture of different situations, demands, decisions in which faith has expressed itself, which cannot be reduced to some doctrine of justification. It is questionable whether Luke has understood the Pauline interest in it. At least, the Lukan report of Paul's sermon in Antioch that "by him [Jesus] every one that believes is freed from everything from which you could not be freed by the law of Moses" sounds as if justification by faith were merely an additional help, if and when the obedience to the law did not suffice (Acts 13:38–39).

It is true that Luke does not provide us a clear concept of *heilsgeschichte,* a distinct Christology, or a precise soteriology. He is far from the Matthean presentation of continuity and difference between law and gospel, from the Johannine picture of Jesus revealing himself as the unique son of God, and from the Pauline concentration on justification by faith in the crucified Jesus. Luke is, therefore, not especially helpful in times of conflict, when it is necessary for the church to formulate its position as precisely as possible and to draw the borders as clearly as possible against indefensible errors. But has not the Matthean pattern of *heilsgeschichte* led to the abominable persecutions of the Jews? It has become an instrument in the hands of persons, many of whom were even subjectively devoted Christians, which seemed to enable them to understand God's way in the *heilsgeschichte,* leading away from the disobedient Jews to the obedient Christians. And have not John and Paul been used excessively in gnosticism, in which the heavenly Christ and his meaning for the understanding of human existence became so dominant that Jesus disappeared more and more, until "Christ" meant nothing more than a symbol of divine grace and could easily be replaced by Attis or Osiris or any other mythical figure? Their Christology and soteriology have become an instrument in the hands of persons, many of whom were even subjectively devoted Christians, by which they mastered the living God and imprisoned him in a system of thoughts of human existence which remains basically the same in all centuries and on all continents, in all cultures and religions. Without obliterating Luke's deficiencies, we have to see him against the background of these developments. Then his positive contribution to the message of the New Testament becomes clear. What, eventually, is it?

4. Luke's understanding of the passion of Jesus

Instead of Mark's word about Jesus' death as a ransom for many (10:45), Luke reports a saying on "the Son of man who came to seek and to save the lost" (19:10) and especially the word of Jesus at the table of his last supper on earth: "I am among you as the one who serves" (22:27). The suggestion that, in the understanding of Luke, the crucifixion of Jesus was but a deplorable mishap is out of question. Much more than Mark, Luke points in the second half of Jesus' ministry to the coming passion. Moses and Elijah foretell his "departure" in Jerusalem (9:31). His journey to Jerusalem, mentioned time and again from 9:51 on, is the journey to his decease. The term used in 9:51 means his death, though it may imply also his ascension.[33] In 9:44 Luke is satisfied with the prediction of rejection and suffering without adding that of resurrection, as Mark does at this place. The same is true for Luke's redactional interpolation of 17:25 into the eschatological sermon of Jesus. Luke points also to the uniqueness of Jesus' death in his presentation of the parable of the vineyard tenants. He differs from Mark and Matthew in the fact that, according to him, the servants are not killed, but only the son. The prospect on the "baptism" that Jesus has to undergo on the cross is peculiar to the third gospel (12:50), and 13:33 states the necessity of his journey to his death: "It cannot be that a prophet should perish away from Jerusalem." The scandal of the cross is stressed by Luke's emphasis on the blindness of the twelve who understand neither the fact that it will come nor its purpose or sense.

Luke does not provide us with a formula which would enable

us to cope with this scandal so that it would cease to be a scandal, once we understood its meaning. The death on the cross, definitely in sight on Jesus' last evening, is the climax of his serving by which he seeks and saves the lost. Shortly after this word about his serving, Jesus quotes Isaiah 53: "He was reckoned with transgressors" (22:37), and this is fulfilled when he is crucified between two criminals, a fact that Luke emphasizes repeatedly. This is typical. The death of Jesus is an event in history which cannot be reduced to any all-embracing formula, be it that of ransom or atonement or justification. The story of the death of Jesus must be told, but one needs a full understanding of all the stories of the Gospels to know what it means "to seek and save the lost" or "to serve." This is expressed in the parables of the lost sheep, coin, and son, in the figures of the praying Pharisee and publican, in the comparison of the two debtors, also in Luke's tendency to give prominence to women,[34] and especially in the passion story: in the healing of the ear of the high priest's servant and in the words of the dying Jesus praying for his torturers and promising paradise to the criminal. It means different things for different people: judgment that calls one back from a wrong way of life, encouragement for another that helps the individual to continue on his or her difficult road, reunion with God for a third that gives the assurance of God's love.

As human life can never be condensed into one formula, neither can the totality of Jesus' serving. Therefore the narrative is the only category in which the death of Jesus on the cross can be proclaimed. The whole life of Jesus is the context which interprets what his death means, and without which it cannot be rightly understood. To it belongs Jesus' authority to heal the sick as well as his weakness on the cross; his fellowship with publicans and prostitutes as well as his rejection by his contemporaries even after his first sermon; the miracle of the birth as well as his rebuff of all demands for signs; his parables about God seeking the lost as well as his proclamations of judgment with their woes. The report on this life starts with strongly accentuated stories about the conception, the birth, and the childhood of Jesus. It is not about a hero whose activity should be imitated but much more about a life in which the grace of God becomes manifest, not less in the passive beginning and end than in the active teaching and working of his ministry. It is remarkable that the story of the annunciation of Jesus' birth follows verse by verse, and often literally, that of the annunciation of John's birth. But the first paragraph, which speaks about the piety and righteousness of John's parents, is missing in the case of Mary. Moreover, in the first story Zechariah is the grammatical subject: "He was serving as priest . . . etc.," and it is only three verses later that the angel is introduced as the object of his seeing. Quite differently, the second story starts with the angel, and Mary appears only in the second verse as the goal of his mission. Mary and her child are, from the beginning, totally dependent on God's act and thus symbols of the total grace of God. Therefore the story ends with Mary's answer: "I am the handmaid of the Lord; let it be to me according to your word." She does not need the proving sign of God, as Zechariah does; she will see it only later when visiting her kinswoman.

5. Contingent earthly history as God's history

However, granted that the history of Jesus' life and death is meaningful history and that it means different things for different people, is Luke able to distinguish this history as the presence of God from all other meaningful history? Can he express in an understandable way its unique importance for all people of all times and places? We started with the old problem of how seemingly contingent history, related to a specific time and a specific place, can be proclaimed as absolute truth. We may grant to Luke that he lets us understand the Christ-event as being real history within a certain realm of time and place. But can he say that this is "eschatological" history, a history which changes the world and human existence in it definitely, even beyond the end of this world and this life?

There are experiences of God's guidance which change our lives, perhaps for an hour or a day or up to our death. Of such experiences the Psalmists tell: in his illness the author has been helped, and this made him praise God and trust in him. Perhaps this is an individual experience which does not go beyond oneself; perhaps one tells it to others, as is done in the Psalms. There are other experiences which become relevant for a whole country or a

whole generation. This is true for the election of the prophet
Jeremiah. If it had not been written down, its influence would have
died soon after his death or, at least, after some generations. But
there are also experiences which remain the basis of all life within a
given realm, even before they enter the human consciousness. The
call to Abraham, the escape of Israel through the Red Sea, the capture of the land of promise remain the basis of Israel's life. There
would be no Israel without these experiences, and all Israelites are
born into this history of God experienced by their fathers, whether
they know about it or not. But as the history after the exile and,
specifically, the history of Jesus shows, it is only to the Israelites'
good if they learn to understand God's aim in letting this happen.
This means that, in Luke's understanding, what we usually call the
Christ-event belongs to this last category so that it is the all-embracing final experience of God's saving love. It is not basically different
from other experiences, but it is God's definite "visit and redemption" (1:68) and therefore unique.

6. Israel and Jesus

So, we ask: What is the relation of the Christ-event, first,
to the history of Israel, second, to the history of the church? On the
one hand, we have seen that it was Luke who, in the parable of the
vineyard tenants, stressed the uniqueness of the death of Jesus, its
final and definite importance set against all experiences of the
prophets of Israel. The same is achieved by his frequent references
to the Scriptures which come to their fulfillment in the destiny of
Jesus, especially in his (otherwise inconceivable) death. On the other
hand, we have also seen that this is not a *heilsgeschichte* in the same
sense as there is a line in Old Testament history leading up to an
end, which is only understandable as the final climax of a long development. Surprisingly enough, the childhood stories do not reach
for holy history in order to introduce the coming of Jesus, but to the
history of a casually selected contemporary couple and their experiences. They are certainly very similar to those of Sarah, Rachel, the
wife of Manoah, and Hannah; all the more is it typical in that it is
contemporary history with which that of Mary and Jesus is inter-
laced. This underlines the basic sameness of the experience of God

by pious Israelites of the Old Testament period and by the witnesses of the life and death of Jesus. At the same time, the Jesus story is put up to a plainly higher level. Even more, it is only the Jesus story which gives its meaning to the story of John and his parents. The long waiting of Elizabeth for the birth of her child only makes sense in that he will be the forerunner of the one for whom all devoted Israelites had waited for centuries.

There is a continuity, of which Paul would never speak, from Old Testament piety, even observance of the law, to New Testament faith. Paul describes the eschatological newness of the time by clearly distinguishing New Testament justification by faith from the life under the law, in which humans tried to build up their own righteousness. Luke sees it differently. There are those who think that they are righteous (18:9) or pretend to be so (20:20; cf. 15:1–2; 16:15); they stand in sharp opposition to Jesus and cannot understand him. This is what Paul would say of those who "pursue the righteousness which is based on law" and thus "seek to establish their own righteousness" (Rom. 9:31; 10:3). But those who are really righteous, as the law taught them, are according to Luke poor and wanting people who are waiting with empty hands for God's coming salvation; an old couple without children and therefore without any earthly future; a young girl in an obscure small Galilean town; an old man with very little time left to him; a widow with 84 years of a solitary life behind her. Even the predominance of women is significant. Zechariah grows dumb, whereas Elizabeth greets and praises the coming Messiah. Joseph appears merely as an attribute of Mary and has nothing to do with the birth of the Messiah, whereas Mary proves to be the handmaid of God whom all generations will call blessed. Simeon is ready to depart after his prophecy, whereas Hannah speaks of the Messiah to all who are looking for the redemption of Jerusalem. Basically this is what Paul would say of Abraham: He believed in God "who gives life to the dead and calls into existence the things that do not exist," and "he believed against hope" (Rom. 4:17–18). Neither would Paul deny that there were always some in Israel who lived in that faith of Abraham, the "seven thousand men who have not bowed the knee to Baal" (11:4). The difference between Paul and Luke lies in the emphasis of Paul on the new understanding of oneself as justified by the grace of God and not by one's own accomplishments, whereas Luke sees in the manifold experiences of Israel God's training towards a faith which expects everything from God and will, therefore, be open to God's definite visit in Jesus Christ (1:68, 78; 7:16; 19:44; Acts 15:14).

This visit is, in Luke, "eschatological," final and all-embracing not in the sense that it is without any analogy, like a meteor falling down from the sky. It is not even the case that analogies are only to be found in the holy history of biblical times. They are to be seen in the story of a contemporary family. It is eschatological in the sense that it fulfills all former experiences by giving them their sense. As the long waiting for a child of Elizabeth finds its meaning in the birth of Jesus, so all the joyous and sad experiences of similar kind in Israel's history find their goal in him. The same is true for the destinies of all the prophets in Israel who met rejection and death in fulfilling their task. This would be totally senseless if Jesus had not ended this long line of suffering and proved that just in this way God's saving visit to his people took place. Luke has separated Jesus' word about Jerusalem killing the prophets from the word of the Wisdom about sending prophets, whom they will "kill and crucify," which form one saying in Matthew 23:34–39, and has put it into the context of Jesus' journey to Jerusalem, where all the prophets must die (13:33–35).

7. Jesus and the church

This leads to the last and decisive question: How is this life and especially this death of Jesus significant for those who believe in him? We have seen that Luke does not speak of ransom or atonement. It looks as if it were merely an example to be imitated. The prayers of the dying Jesus are repeated by Stephen in his martyrdom (Luke 23:34, 46; Acts 7:59–60). The phrase "the blood of Stephen thy witness was shed" (Acts 22:20) reminds the reader of "the blood of all the prophets [which was] shed" and of Jesus' own "blood shed for you" (Luke 11:50; 22:20). The journey of Paul to Jerusalem is, even in its details, very similar to that of Jesus (Acts 19:21; 20:22; 21:4, 11–15). Paul will "be delivered into the hands of the Gentiles," very much like the Son of man (Acts 21:11; Luke

18:32; 24:7). It is also Luke who inserts the apostles into the long line of the persecuted prophets which finds its goal in the time of Jesus (11:49). Jesus among the disciples is the one who serves in order that they also shall serve (22:24–27), and the rule that we have to enter the kingdom of God "through many tribulations" applies to the church as to Jesus himself (Acts 14:22; Luke 24:26).

And yet this would not suffice. As Luke stresses the uniqueness of Jesus' death over against the destiny of the prophets, he knows that God put his stamp on this one death by raising Jesus from the dead.[35] It is, therefore, the risen Lord who greets his martyr, and it is the hand of his Lord Jesus into which Stephen puts his soul (Acts 7:56, 60). It is the same risen Lord who shows Paul how much he will have to suffer for his name's sake (9:16) and who accompanies him on his journey. Thus he is not merely an example; he is the one who has opened the road, who has broken through the jungle and cleared the path, and who accompanies those who follow him. In Jesus a new possibility of life has flashed up, lived after the will of the creator, in its totality oriented towards God. Therefore it is Jesus who creates "the faith through him" (as Acts 3:16 runs literally) and who "opens the heart" to faith (Acts 16:14). Since this is so, repentance or conversion is not simply a human accomplishment. It is given to the person, and if it is true that Luke likes these terms, it is also true that he wants to say by them that the faith which is given to the person is not a mere idea in his brain, but permeates the whole of his life. It is Luke who tells the Parable of the Lost Sheep, not as a challenge to the believer to go after a lost fellow member of the church, as Matthew 18:10–14 understands it, but as the message of God's seeking. The sheep is totally passive in the story of the parable, and is just so the proper image for the sinner who repents.

If faith cannot be reduced to a mere intellectual acceptance of a *heilsgeschichtlich* pattern or a dogmatic formula or a specific understanding of human existence, which would lead to practical consequences only in a secondary way; and if faith, by necessity, embraces the fullness of life, intellect and sentiment, will and action, heart and senses, then God's saving history must be open to being reexperienced. Believing in Jesus Christ means, according to Luke, more than catching a pattern of God's acting in history which enables humankind to understand all history. It means more than being taught a truth which humans would have to accept in order to be saved. It means more than a convincing view of human existence which would be demonstrated. It means that the church which understands that God has definitely visited his people in Jesus Christ will reexperience the love of God to the sinner, the strength of God given to the weak, the challenge of God filling an empty life with new sense, and the help of God on dangerous journeys. Luke knows that the fullness of God's salvation cannot be confined to one or several historical patterns, to one or several Christological titles, to one or several doctrines; it can only be told in a varied multitude of stories which tell us what experiences to expect when trusting in Jesus Christ.

V.
Jesus Christ in Word and Sacrament

There is a story of a priest and his very economical house-keeper who used to combine all the leftovers of the week for a Saturday night dinner. So when the priest once forgot to say grace, she reminded him: "Won't you say grace first?" "Oh no," he said, "that food has been blessed already three or four times." There may be the danger that it looks like such a Saturday night dinner when we come to the subject of applying our insights into the approach of Luke to the modern dialogue between the Catholics and Protestants. Shall we, notwithstanding, say grace for it, not merely in words which sound good, but in our way of meeting other denominations and of thinking and speaking about them? I do not know the Orthodox Church well enough to discuss its doctrine explicitly; nor do we have the time to take into consideration all the differences between the various Protestant denominations. However, different positions of Orthodox and Protestant churches will be dealt with implicitly when we consider the basic Catholic and Protestant views.

1. Speaking in images

Years ago *Ernst Fuchs,* retired Professor of New Testament in Marburg, said that the only thing New Testament scholars had found out in the last fifty years was the fact that Jesus had spoken in parables. He may have said that tongue in cheek, since this does not seem to be much of a new discovery. And yet, I think, he took it seriously. True, every Christian who has had a minimum of religious instruction knows that Jesus spoke in parables. But we know it as a matter of course, and it is just for this reason that we do not actually realize what it means. The best illustration of what it means that I know (and which I have already used several times) is a German translation of an American novel in which the word "honey" (in the sense of "darling") was translated literally. In German, honey is only the product of the bees. Thus, the translated text ran, as if we would say, "Oh jam, what a dreamlike evening—shall we not go dancing somewhere, jam?" This shows that as soon as we use imagery, even something as common as "honey," a machine can no longer cope with the text. When we say "dinner at seven," a computer can translate it into German or French. When we say "honey," it is at the end of its possibilities. Imagery cannot be understood mechanically but needs a human interpreter.

This goes much deeper, and here we owe a lot to American scholars. It was *Amos Wilder* who has, as early as 1964, understood the parable as an expanded metaphor which does not only teach something about reality but also lets the hearer participate in it.[36] In 1973 *J. D. Crossan* said of the metaphor: "It gives absolutely no information until after the hearer has entered into it and experienced it from inside itself."[37] This is certainly true. Even if we succeeded in building a computer which could check the context in order to choose between two different German terms, it would not be sufficient. What a range of possible meanings lies in the word "honey." The ardent love of a young boy may express itself in this word when he dares to say it for the first time to his girl (the reader realizes that I look sometimes at films produced in the thirties!). Or it may mean nothing at all when the girl in the department store asks me: "What do you want, honey?" Only a human person who is moved by what the other wants to convey can understand what it really is that the word expresses. It must stir up some feeling in the hearer, otherwise it remains incomprehensible. If someone had never felt anything like love, the exclamation of the boy would simply sound crazy. That means, and this is an extremely important result, that a parable can never be handed down mechanically, but only by hearers who let themselves be engaged by its message. Like a good joke, a parable happens whenever it conveys to hearers something they have experienced formerly in order to lead them further on to new experience.

This does not imply that a good parable or a good image is less precise than a direct statement. On the contrary, when I say of a lady "she is icy," this is not literally true—her temperature will be around 37 degrees Centigrade. And yet it is much more apt than saying "she has difficulties of contact, she does not consider the feelings of others, she is sexually frigid" (which, by the way, is also an image). It is the modern scientist who detected that even in natural science we are forced to think and to speak in images which sometimes are contradictory in order to get as near to truth as possible.[38]

2. Jesus speaking in parables

What does this mean with respect to Jesus' parables? Here again we owe much to American scholars. *R. W. Funk* emphasized that in his parables Jesus came into the world of his hearers, that he refused to sum up his parables in any ready-to-wear formula, that they were models of reality and interpreted by the whole work of Jesus.[39] *N. Perrin* gave us a very helpful survey on the development of the research and stressed, as *Dan O. Via* had already done,[40] the relation of the parables to Jesus' view of the kingdom of God which is as well a present as a future reality.[41] An Italian, *T. Aurelio,* using the term of *I.T. Ramsey,* called the parables "events of disclosure," in which Jesus discloses himself.[42] In Germany it is, first of all, *E. Jüngel,*[43] in France, *P. Ricoeur*[44] who continued on the road which Fuchs had opened.[45]

We shall follow some of these suggestions, though very briefly. First, Jesus comes into the area of our experiences. He enters the world of the small Galilean farmer with his anxiety about the harvest, of the father with his uneasiness about his son's way of life, of the wedding guests with their joy. This implies that God is not simply somewhere else, outside of our world in his heaven, but that he is to be met in our earthly lives. Secondly, it means that, strictly speaking, God cannot be taught but he can be experienced. Teaching may be extremely important, as we have seen, in a negative way, to save our experiences from going astray, and in a positive way, to direct them towards a real understanding. But "teaching" in itself does not convey the living God. It may even hinder his coming, though it may be totally correct. It is exactly the most correct and orthodox teaching that would suggest that we had got hold of God. Then he can no longer come in his surprising ways. It was correct and orthodox to teach the law of Moses as the word of God, and yet it made people blind for the one in whom the obedience to the law of Moses reached, in an unexpected way, its absolute climax.

This is true in a three-fold way. There are parables which tell about God and his kingdom, sin and reconciliation, heaven and hell. It is even true that Jesus almost always spoke in parables when touching these topics. If the function of a parable were merely to illustrate his teaching, as a teacher would illustrate the fact that 8 divided by 4 is 2 by using the example of 4 boys sharing 8 apples, Jesus would give us the meaning of a parable before or after telling it, in a direct statement. But even if this has occasionally been done by those who handed it down, the most Jesus himself added was an introductory sentence that the story had something in common with the kingdom of God. He absolutely refused to sum it up in a dogmatic formula which the hearer could carry home, confident that he or she now possessed the truth. Then there are parables that Jesus told in the past tense, but which seem to say something about the future. But it is not even clear whether they mean a future experience or decision within a person's earthly life or a future beyond the end of this world. Similarly, Jesus refused to give to his hearers a *heilsgeschichtlich* timetable that they could carry home, confident that nothing unexpected could happen to them. Finally, there are parables which tell of very amoral behavior, like that of the dishonest steward or that of the unrighteous judge. And again, Jesus avoided giving his hearers an existential pattern that they could simply carry home to imitate.

The parables asked for an answer, and the answer could be given only in dogmatic or historical or ethical categories. Thus neither dogmatic formulae nor *heilsgeschichtlich* patterns nor ethical models are wrong. But all hearers had to give their answers in their own language. For one it meant to see the special election of Israel and to "go nowhere among the Gentiles" (Matt. 10:5), for another—or even for the same one in a later period—it meant to realize that God was also the God of the Gentiles and to praise him for that (Acts 11:17–18). For one it meant to see the kingdom of God present in Jesus (Luke 17:21), for another to watch for its coming (Matt. 25:13). For one it meant to leave his family (Matt. 8:22), for another to go home (Mark 5:19). Again, this had nothing to do with being vague. What the parable means is very clear and precise for every hearer who has ears to hear (Mark 4:9).

3. Luke, the storyteller

This is what Luke understood, perhaps better than his fellow evangelists. He is very reluctant to use doctrinal formulae or *heilsgeschichtlich*-apocalyptic patterns or even existential examples. Why? If Rev. X meets someone who has had bad experiences with the church and thinks he or she knows what a minister is and thinks ministers preach some untrue ideals there are difficulties for the meeting, if the other knows Rev. X's profession. Rev. X may succeed in a long discussion to overcome the prejudices; but even then the whole evening is predetermined by the image the other person had of a minister. Instead of presenting the self as it really is, the minister has to fight against this wrong image and cannot introduce the subjects really important to him or her. If the person with the prejudices does not know who his partner is the minister may make such a good impression that towards midnight the prejudiced person will ask: "What kind of work are you in?" In this case he may tell his friend next morning: "You know, Mr. or Mrs. X is really a minister." By then "minister" has become the prejudiced person's own term and means something totally different from what it had meant the day before. In this way the first Christians may have said: "You know, Jesus is really the Christ," but "Christ" meant something totally different from the general meaning of "minister," so the living and dying and rising Jesus determined the meaning of "Christ" for the first Christians.

Therefore Luke uses Christological titles more or less at random, and various doctrinal explications side by side without clearly discerning between right and wrong. But he tells us a lot about Jesus, his birth, his life, his death, his resurrection, his work in the church. Titles and doctrines just indicate the dimension in which he is to be seen. They all point to the central fact that in him God visits the world. But none of them is able to catch the truth. It needs the whole lot of very different stories and parables and sermons to bring the living Jesus to the hearer.

What Jesus achieved by using parables, Luke did by telling stories without giving his readers easy solutions to all the riddles presented by them. Thus he forces his readers to let themselves be moved by his stories, to ask their own questions, and to arrive at their own answers. As it is impossible to catch the totality of a living person in one or even in several snapshots, it is even much more impossible to catch the living God in one or several formulae or patterns. As one needs at least a film to describe what a living person really is, so it needs at least a full gospel with numerous stories and reports of Jesus' whole activity and destiny to show who he is.

This secures the *extra nos*, the fact that God can never be identified with our own ideas, feelings, performances, that he comes from outside of ourselves into our lives. At the same time, it secures the *pro nobis*, the fact that God can only be understood as the one who loves us, who meets us, who calls us. When Luke tells his stories, he tells them in the past tense and of a foreign country. God has acted "outside of us," and this is even true for the contemporaries in Galilee (13:26–27). When Luke omits giving an interpretation that one could appropriate and make one's own, he forces his reader to be moved by his narrative in an ever new way and to read his text as written "for him." How does this affect the discussion which is going on between the churches?

4. The Protestant churches
The strength and the danger of the Protestant churches is their concentration on the Word. It is the word of God which brings the person salvation, and it is by faith alone that one accepts the grace of God. Grace does not become a new quality of the believer but is strictly the quality of God's judgment over humanity, the famous "gratia imputata" of the Reformers. The individual, as sinner, *is* righteous because of God's word, which justifies him or her, not because of a change of his or her life.

However, what is this word of God which faith accepts? How can people get hold of it? It is in the area of Protestantism that the historico-critical method has been born and used extensively. It brought not only the philological aids to deal with Hebrew and Greek texts, but also clear criteria for the work of the historian.

First, one must start with a critical mind, always doubting the evidence, until it can be verified (Ernst Troeltsch's "Kritik"). Secondly, one achieves this verification by comparing a questioned event with analogous events the historicity of which is established (the "Analogie"). Thirdly, one puts it into the context of the general history of a given period (the "Korrelation").[46] In such a way reason can master the problems of history at least up to a reasonable degree of certitude. On the one hand, this has led to modern neo-positivism, which accepts, for an academic approach, nothing but facts that can be verified according to such criteria. On the other hand, it opened up a much more influential and helpful way, that of existential interpretation, in which the content of the biblical word, as analyzed by the historico-critical method, appears as a new understanding of human existence. The historical facts in the Bible are often without analogies in other areas of history (such as the miracles), and not easily correlated with the general history of the time. This is especially true of the resurrection of Jesus. But their historicity remains, by and large, irrelevant for existential understanding. Paul, who allegedly knew almost nothing about Jesus of Nazareth, becomes then, with his doctrine of justification, *the* center of the New Testament. One should have been a bit more critical, though, for the author of the Johannine letters almost certainly knew the Gospel of John. Whether he had written it himself or not, nonetheless we hear nothing whatsoever about the earthly ministry of Jesus, and none of his sayings are quoted. This is less than we find in Paul's letters, which presuppose at least in the liturgy of the Lord's Supper some knowledge of the last night in which Jesus was betrayed (1 Cor. 11:23), or, in a recommendation of the collection for Jerusalem, the knowledge of Jesus having been poor (2 Cor. 8:9), or, in quite a number of ethical admonitions, some general knowledge of Jesus' teaching and some literal reminiscences of his sayings.

Be this as it may, the gnostic misunderstanding of Paul's position shows its danger clearly, and gnosticism is not limited to the second and third century A.D. Paul's doctrine of justification could easily be transformed into an existential philosophy which would no longer need Jesus. It needed but the "word," and the word could be systematized and preserved in a doctrine of justification or an existential system which individuals could make their own. One might still know that Jesus was the first one to approach life in this way, but it was Paul who caught it in a reflected and systematic form, and it is the modern philosopher who transforms it into a modern way of understanding one's own existence. Jesus is no longer necessary.

The ethical level, strength, and danger of a Protestant concentration on the word, and especially on the doctrine of justification becomes clear. It liberates the believer from all legalistic observance of the law and gives the believer the freedom of making decisions. At the same time, it robs persons of all the signposts which could direct the way and of the barriers which could save persons from getting lost. In modern *situationsethik* Augustine's famous word is quoted in a distorted way: "Just love, and then do whatever you want," whereas the Church Father meant: "Love [using the word for God's love to us which becomes charity in us], and what you want [to do in this orientation towards God], achieve it."[47] Thus Jesus and his way of life can be replaced by the ever-changing situation and its necessities.

5. The Catholic churches

The strength and the danger of the Catholic churches is their concentration on the Sacrament. The sacrament cannot be obtained in every library like the word of God, the Bible. It is therefore the connection with the church, the communion of all believers, which saves humanity. The sacrament of baptism incorporates man and/or woman into the church and gives them a new quality, and the sacrament of the eucharist keeps them in the body of Christ. The grace of God is not merely a verdict of not guilty spoken by the heavenly judge, a *gratia imputata*; it is actually infused into one as a divine power or as a new quality which enables the believer to live in a new way. It is *gratia infusa*.

There is, of course, no historico-critical or any other scientific method to analyze the sacrament. Its secret is founded in the words of institution spoken, according to the tradition of the church, by the Lord himself, taught and interpreted by his church. Therefore, it is the church's authority which gives to the sacrament its divine quality. Whereas in many Protestant churches a group of laypeople can celebrate the Lord's Supper, even if no ordained minister is present, this is impossible in the Catholic understanding. Even if, on the one hand, other Protestant churches stress the necessity of a good church order which urges their members not to celebrate the Lord's Supper without an ordained minister, though it would be basically possible, and if, on the other hand, some Catholic churches would admit that in a case of emergency (in a concentration camp for instance) something like a eucharist without a priest might be possible, the gulf between the positions is very wide here. I do not see how it could be bridged today, because the understanding of what the office of a priest in the church means differs totally between the official Catholic doctrine and the positions at least of some Protestant churches.[48]

It is in the area of Catholicism that the pattern of *heilsgeschichte* was emphasized recently. Since the church can never be totally deprived of its right understanding of God's ways, and since this church is the one Catholic Church visible in its authorities, in the pope, the bishops, and the priests, the guidance of God can be traced in the history of the Catholic Church despite all its errors and detours. There is, as Karl Rahner formulated, an official, pure, "churchly" *heilsgeschichte*. This leads to a further extension of this idea, to the fascinating attempt to draw a picture of a divine evolution of world and humanity. By it the visible effects of the grace of God could be traced in the history of nature and perhaps even in that of humankind. Thus faith could get hold of God's action in the process of nature and in the guidance of human lives.

Again, the difficulties become enormous. Dostoyevsky's arch inquisitor has posed the questions. Could a church which possesses the truth and also the authority of binding and loosing not dispense with Jesus? And what is his role within a fixed pattern of evolution? Does he simply reveal the trend of this process? And is God, then, more than the law of nature? Or if so, is Jesus the guarantee for a trust in the continuing progress of world and humanity, perhaps even in a guaranteed final salvation of all beings?

On the ethical level, the church helps its believers by some clear rules and by the institution of a father confessor. This combines the system of unchangeable laws, even detailed prescriptions for a Christian behavior, with their adaptation to a modern situation. Again, the dangers of this way are obvious. Does it not lead into a new legalism? Do not the unchangeable laws hinder the responsible decisions which have become unavoidable in a totally changed world?

6. Luke's contribution to a modern ecumenical dialogue

When we now turn to Luke again, we realize that he possesses no kerygma in the sense of a formula into which the whole truth could be pressed. Even the word "gospel" appears only in Acts 15:7 and 20:24, whereas Mark, writing not much more than a quarter of what Luke wrote, uses it eight times. However, the verb "to proclaim the gospel" (literally "to gospel") is frequent in Luke's writings. This is typical. The gospel is, for him, an event, the living word of God, which may come to people in ever new and unexpected ways, not so much as a message which could be definitely put into one or several sentences to be handed down as the unchangeable truth. Nor does Luke possess a clear pattern of *heilsgeschichte* or of a church order. The number of apostles, twelve, seems to be important to him at the beginning of the church (Acts 1:22), but when James died, he was not replaced (12:2). There is a continuity with the twelve tribes of Israel and with Jesus' choice of twelve disciples during his earthly ministry which has to be expressed, but not a binding church order. In the same way, the continuity between the old covenant and the new one had to be manifested by two Jerusalem delegates coming to Samaria (8:14), but even then, and most certainly later on, Luke gives no hint to any superiority of the church of Jerusalem over other churches. On the contrary, he knows of the collection of Paul for the Jerusalem church among the Gentile-Christian congregations (Acts 24:17). Historically seen, this was part of the agreement between the apostles in Jerusalem and Paul, very important to both parties (Gal. 2:10; Rom. 15:26; 1 Cor. 16:1–4; 2 Cor. 8–9). It was something parallel to the temple tax paid by all Jews wherever they were living or the "Peter's pence" in the medieval church, and it may have been understood as a kind of subjection of the Gentile-Christian churches to the mother church in Jerusalem or at least as its official recognition. But Luke gives no space to this collection in his book; he even replaces it by a spontaneous money-raising drive against a coming famine, suggested charismatically by a prophet (Acts 11:27–30). This shows how little Luke is interested in a hierarchial order of the one church. Nor does Luke advocate an apostolic succession. True, Paul and Barnabas appoint elders in southern Asia Minor (14:23); but in his farewell speech to the elders of Ephesus, which forms a kind of programmatic view of the future of the church, Paul mentions only the Holy Spirit that has made them guardians of the church (20:28), and he says nothing about the doctrine of the church, but only about their exemplary moral behavior. Moreover, Paul himself is no apostle in Acts (except in Luke's tradition in 14:4, 14 where he and Barnabas are called so as "missionaries"). He is not even ritually confirmed by the twelve; it was a common member of the church, called by a prophetic vision, who laid his hands upon him (9:10–19).

Luke tells stories about Jesus and stories which show how they came to life again in the post-Easter church, how faith came into being, in words and deeds, in joy and suffering, in courage and temptation. There may be a kind of kerygma in the speeches of Peter, Stephen, and Paul, but how very different it is according to the audience. There may be a pattern of conversion to Jesus, but again, how very different does it appear according to the circumstances. Thus Luke warns an extreme Protestantism against the danger of gnosticism. The concentration on a doctrine of justification which has merely to be accepted is far from the fullness of Luke's tradition of all the stories about Jesus. And if Protestantism avoids this danger by emphasis on faith, including its inward sentiments and its outward deeds of charity, it may fall out of the frying pan into the fire. Such a concentration of the phenomenon of faith is far from the fullness of Luke's tradition about so many and so different reactions which Jesus himself brought to life in his disciples. And Luke warns an extreme Catholicism against the way of a new legalism. The concentration on the visible authority of the church is far from the unsystematic fullness in which, according to Luke, the Spirit let Jesus Christ come to life in the church. And if Catholicism avoids this danger by emphasis on a continuous ecclesiastical interpretation of the old doctrines, falling into the fire is not yet excluded. Just changing the flowers or the draping of the cover over a corpse does not vivify it. The manna which was kept for the following morning bred worms and became foul and stinking (Exod. 16:20). A church office which has not only to know but also to declare in a way which becomes visible even in the printed sentences of a press report, about who is teaching inside or outside of the realm of salvation, is far from the fullness of Luke's stories about the ever new listening to the directions of God of the first Christians.[49]

As no one can ever define the meaning of a parable of Jesus definitely so that the parable itself would become superfluous, so no one can put aside the richness of Jesus' ministry and his coming to life again in the church, as if a kerygmatic summary of what it means for human existence or an authorized statement or office of a church would suffice. As the parable of Jesus may suddenly point to some forgotten but important part of the gospel, so the Lukan stories may time and again start to speak in quite unexpected ways. They point both to God's action outside of us, of our time and our country, and to its character of a part of contingent history which cannot be changed into a timeless statement, be it a doctrine or a concept of *heilsgeschichte*.

7. An ecumenical eucharist

We may check these suggestions with regard to the understanding of the eucharist. Here the Protestant danger is the retreat to the Word. The sacrament becomes a merely symbolic confirmation of what the Word has proclaimed. In this case, it becomes more and more irrelevant. Modern persons, no longer in need of mystical symbols, need no such corroboration of the Word which they heard and accepted intellectually. This leads to the Protestant scandal that the eucharist, if it is celebrated at all on this Sunday, becomes a negligible appendage at the end of the central service of the Word, after which a large part of the congregation has left the church. It is not the Protestant doctrine of the Lord's Supper but the practice which is so alarming. The Catholic danger is a one-sided concentration on the elements and their transubstantiation or whatever takes its place in more modern Catholic dogmatics. They seem to give a guarantee of a material, though invisible, presence of God. Again it is not so much the doctrine which is scandalous but the practice of an adoration of the elements outside of the event of the eucharist. Modern doctrine interprets it as remembrance of what has been given in the last eucharist and as trusting hope of the next one, but the popular practice often comes close to belief in magical charms.

Luke reminds his Protestant readers of the fact that no formula or doctrine or existential pattern can ever hand down the wealth of life that the totality of Jesus' teaching and acts implies. God cannot be imprisoned in even the most correct description of faith or of its content. He meets us in very contingent happenings within our time and history because he met us, once for all, in the very contingent happenings of life and death of Jesus of Nazareth. God meeting us today means more than having his Word. It always implies the time and the place in which we hear it, the sentiment and feeling in which we hear, the outward occasion and the inward openness to hear it, and a thousand other things. Therefore God's coming in the eucharist, including the eating and drinking of bread and wine given to one individually and yet within a table fellowship, cannot simply be replaced by hearing the Word.

Luke reminds his Catholic readers of the fact that God met us in the historical events of Jesus' life and death, not in any static object. God cannot be imprisoned in any correctly repeated rite, let alone in its elements. His coming also takes the very contingent situation in which he finds us very seriously. It is not merely he and I who are present in the event of the eucharist but also the company of my fellow guests at table that becomes important, and not less my contact to the society at large within which I am celebrating the eucharist. The South American churches know perhaps better than any others of that importance and the situation in its fullness is that in which we eat and drink.

Against Protestant and Catholic misunderstandings we are to aspire to a celebration of the eucharist in which the real presence of the living Lord is neither reduced to a confessional statement nor to a mysteriously transformed matter, but is to be found in the wholeness of the celebration, in its prayers, its hymns, its teaching, its table fellowship which accompany the distribution of bread and wine and the eating and drinking. This presupposes a form in which the fellowship is not merely to be believed against all appearances. There should be, at least, the occasion for real fellowship from person to person. At the same time, prayers, hymns, and the proclamation of the Word must make unambiguously clear that such table fellowship is a given one, founded in the fellowship which God grants us. The central part of eating and drinking bread and wine should manifest both—the character of God's grace given "vertically from above" and its manifestation within our earthly situation.

As described by Luke, even more than the other evangelists, Jesus entered in a seemingly casual way the table fellowship of an everyday meal in order to perform the miracle of all miracles, namely to reintegrate a publican or even a prostitute into the fellowship with God. Jesus, as Luke again, more emphatically than the other evangelists, describes him, ate on his last evening on earth the passover meal with his disciples. He spoke explicitly of his longing for that fellowship and gave, by his speech after the meal and distribution of the cup, a visible and audible expression to this fellowship to which God bound them together by appointing his kingdom to Jesus in order that he might appoint it to his disciples (Luke 22:15–30). On this very occasion he taught them to see him as their Lord serving them (vs. 27). His serving, however, did not start at the beginning of the meal and finish at its end, but was part of his serving in his whole ministry before and in its climax on the cross after this meal. Thus again the wealth of all the stories about his deeds, the reports of his sermons, and the narrative of his crucifixion which we find in Luke's Gospel becomes present in the focus of the last meal. When God raised Jesus from the dead he put his seal on this serving. Therefore whenever and wherever the church celebrates this meal, he is present as the living Lord who serves us and sends his disciples to serve others. It is the total experience of this meal and of the deeds arising out of this common meal in which the experience of God's fellowship with people is renewed time and again, until it reaches its final goal when Jesus' disciples may eat and drink at his table in his kingdom (vs. 30).

It is certainly not wrong to try to express the truth of the gospel in a title, a formula, a doctrine. We need them urgently in times of conflict with false prophets. It is not wrong to reflect on God's acts in history. We must realize what God wants to teach us in church history about his will for the future. It is not wrong to look for examples of Christian existence and to recognize its patterns. We need them when dealing with the individual, social, and political problems of our lives. As long as we are on earth, we cannot miss the second room with the "lectures about heaven." But we need even more the stories of God's acts in the history of Israel and the church, and, first of all, the stories about Jesus himself. Perhaps they cannot offer us any cut-and-dried solutions or patterns, but they help us to learn from the experience of those they tell about and strike some chords in our lives that sound familiar, so that we get a glimpse into the first room, into heaven itself.

8. God's presence in Jesus Christ and Luke's picture of it[50]

There is one more question to be asked. How far is the Lukan picture of Jesus as the Christ identical with Jesus of Nazareth? Is Luke's claim that in this Jesus God himself has visited his people buttressed by what we know about him?

VI.
God's Presence in Jesus Christ

When our daughter Elizabeth was about three years old we were living in a house on a steep slope. Looking out of the window of the living room you saw the road some fifty feet down. Thus Elizabeth knew that she was not allowed to look through the open window without being held by somebody. Now, one day there was a herd of cows coming along the road, all with bells around their necks, and Elizabeth had to see them. When we came down to the living room, she was leaning out of the open window in a fearfully dangerous position, but holding herself by her own collar. Is this not what we constantly do? We are holding ourselves with ever more insurance, armaments, safe investments, and psychological treatments, and all the time we are just holding ourselves, whereas the only decisive question is whether there is somebody else who holds us. Are we still able to speak of the one who would really hold us? Or are we no longer able to speak about God, since this word conveys thousands of different ideas, or even no ideas at all, to those to whom we speak? What do we really mean when we say "God"?

1. Who is God?

I shall start from some experiences I have had in the last few years. One of my university colleagues in the faculty of medicine declared, not long ago, in a discussion with students of an institute of technology that he was a scientist and would, therefore, approach this question naturally from a scientific point of view. In that case there was, in his view, no doubt that God existed. He would agree that there were some people who did not believe so, but, within the history of humanity, the percentage of those who thought there was no God would be so small that a scientist would have to disregard it, since to every natural law a scientist could detect there would also be a minimal number of exceptions. Thus the small number of modern atheists would be totally insignificant compared with the billions and billions who had lived from the be-

ginning of humankind and who had always adored God. This would
be just that infinitesimal group of beings that would not behave in
the normal way, and a scientist would have to neglect it. Another
colleague of the same faculty offered a round-trip air ticket to Manila to a skeptic telling him he would not have to pay a cent if he
did not return fully persuaded beyond any reasonable doubt that
inexplicable healing miracles happened there.

Much more important was a discussion with some young physicists whom one of my student assistants brought to an open evening. They started from the thesis that they all took for granted,
that it was impossible to do any meaningful research in modern
physics without reckoning with the work of God in all physical action and, especially, in any evolution. The problem they were interested in was merely whether this God had something to do with
individual human lives. Thus the situation has totally changed compared with that of half a century ago. When I was a university student, almost anyone would have agreed that a divine influence on
the individual soul, and thereby on the attitude and the behavior of
an individual, would be at least thinkable, but that God had nothing to do with the course of nature and physical laws. Finally, I
remember an essay in *Neue Zurcher Zeitung* in which the author
explained that the methods of a theologian and those of a physicist
were actually the same. Neither one could get hold of the object
directly. The physicist has to start from some events that can be
observed with instruments in order to conclude about the facts that
caused these events. Physicists never see directly the whole about
which they teach; they are always forced to work their way back
from what they are able to observe to a hypothesis of what is behind
these events. The method of theologians working their way back
from the experiences of people of all centuries to the one who effect-
ed them would be exactly the same.

Thus is seems that it is again possible to speak of God: God
who can be proved with scientific precision; God who manifests
himself in miracles and in indubitable happenings that we cannot
explain, mysterious and divine to us, as the parapsychologists report
them to us; God who, in the understanding of many young physicists, is a necessary hypothesis without which no significant work

can be done in their field; God who is to be detected by a method equal in its structure to that of any modern scientist. Is God, perhaps, taken much more seriously outside of theology than within the discussion of the experts? Has metaphysical thinking regained its central place beside physical research?

And yet, could we not argue just the opposite, step by step? Maybe it is a small percentage of humanity who did or does not believe in God. But, even granted that this be so, what kind of god or gods is it that they believe in? Moreover, could we not argue in exactly the same way and state the fact that, counted from the beginning of our earth, a very small percentage of humanity would not believe that lightning was the direct effect of a god or demon or angel and that therefore the "hypothesis" of electric potential behind it could be neglected? Might it not be that the idea of an existence of God belonged merely to the pre-scientific period of history and that modern society would no longer need the hypothesis of God acting in the world? And again, if we accept some inexplicable happenings, be it in Manila or in some facts that parapsychologists have investigated and proved, what does this really mean? It shows that there are unknown human powers, usually buried deep down in the psyche, hidden and forgotten, but sometimes bursting out of the depths of the soul. Whether we can ever explain them reasonably or not may be an open question, but, however we answer it, explicable or inexplicable powers in the individual are not identical with God. And if a physicist introduces the idea of God's acting in the course of nature—an attempt which would be plainly refused by many colleagues—if a physicist even declares that without God evolution would not be understandable, would God, in this case, be more than a kind of anonymous and inconceivable natural power? Could we only say that it is directed teleologically (towards a final goal)? Not only in our Bible, but, as far as comparative history of religions shows, almost everywhere the center of interest in religion is exactly God's relation to people and their lives and deaths. As long as such a personal communication between God and humanity is not implied, the hypothesis of a natural power, called God, does not lead us any nearer to the God of the Bible. Finally, though it is true that the method of the scientist on the one hand and that of the theologian on the other became more and more similar to each other, are they the same? The fact of this similarity, relevant and welcome as it is, should certainly not mask the main problem which remains still the same as it was centuries ago. If the scientists do their experiments correctly, they will always get the same results, perhaps with a rate of exceptions which is so minimal that they really can disregard it. Their observations from which they draw their conclusions as to the cause of the happenings that they see will always be the same, if they repeat the same experiment in the same way. If not, they have to change their theory. But if a theologian starts the experiment of prayer, for example, will the theologian be sure of always obtaining the same results or even of always going through the same experiences? Is God not unpredictable? If there is no guarantee of the process of the experiment always being the same, how can we draw conclusions that will be sure in a scientific way?

Thus the quest of God has certainly become alive today. God has become a relevant problem and questions arise from all parts of our society. However, we are as far away from a generally accepted solution as ever, or even more than in former years. Could it just be that both accusers and defendants, believers and unbelievers, promoters of a religious approach and promoters of an atheist approach to solve the riddle of human life are debating the wrong issue? The concept of God as an almighty being, omnipotent and omniscient, eternal, high up in heaven, not touched by human finiteness and transitoriness, desires, and sufferings could indeed be just the projection of some intra-psychic dreams or fears. When we turn now to the New Testament we find there a very surprising, strange, and actually shocking statement. The New Testament declares that God is to be found in a very human life and death which ended on the cross.[51] This basic presupposition of the New Testament is so scandalous that, if we manage to cope with it, we probably have not listened carefully enough to what it implies. We certainly have to try again and again to understand what this basic truth really expresses.

Even the question "Who was Jesus?" would not easily lead to a generally accepted answer. But there would be quite a number of contemporaries, especially among the young generation, who would agree that this question could be meaningful and that it would be possible to find some valid answer, at least to a certain degree. However, we have to ask "Who *is* Jesus *Christ?*" By doing so, we presuppose, first, that he is, in some way, still present, and we presuppose, second, that we cannot deal with this question in a really relevant way without seeing him primarily as the one who is sent by God as his delegate and representative in whom God himself becomes reality among us. When we put the question in this way, it will be more difficult and perhaps impossible to find some consensus and to get an answer which would be accepted by all of us. And yet it is exactly this question which we have to answer.

2. The powerlessness of the almighty God

The confession "Jesus Christ" says primarily that God is not to be found where we expect him to be found. He is to be found in Jesus. Miraculous deeds are reported of Jesus and his apostles, and Luke even emphasizes this side of the ministry of Jesus and his disciples. He reports healings and also the raising from death (Luke 7:11–17; 8:49–56; Acts 9:36–42; 20:9–10) and the stilling of the storm (8:22–25, not, however, the walk over the sea, Mark 6:48–50). There is no doubt that, especially in the understanding of Luke, God's power manifests itself in the healing and helping of Jesus, often in an extraordinary way. And yet these reports have to be shielded time and again against all possible misunderstandings of Jesus as being a miracle worker. These healings are certainly one aspect of God's presence in the ministry of Jesus, but not the pivotal one. The real face of God or his innermost heart is to be seen elsewhere.

This becomes especially clear in Mark, which is probably the oldest Gospel. He actually opposes, by the very structure of his Gospel, a view of Jesus as the mighty miracle worker. It is the repeated rejection of Jesus by the Pharisees and Herodians (3:6), by his fellow citizens (6:1–6), by his own incomprehending disciples (8:14–21) and the repeated prediction of his definite rejection in Jerusalem (8:31–32; 9:31–32; 10:32–34) that structure his Gospel.[52] Something very similar happens in the writing of Matthew when he emphasizes the rejection of Jesus by his own people, by God's elected nation, from the very beginning in 2:1–18 to the end in 27:25 and 28:11–15. The trend is less clear in the Fourth Gospel, though its author knows about the ambiguity of miracles (for instance, 6:15, 26; 9:24–25) and a faith which believes without seeing (20:29). Paul has doubtless focused his message on the scandal and the folly of the crucifixion of Jesus, though he has also experienced the spirit and the power of God (1 Cor. 1:23; 2:4–5). Against the one-sided enthusiasm of Corinthians with its emphasis on extraordinary, miraculous gifts of the Spirit, he "decided to know nothing among you except Jesus Christ and him crucified" (2:2). He has learned that his strength lies exactly in his weakness, and that this is true for Jesus himself as it is for his apostle (2 Cor. 13:4; 12:10). This means that God is to be found primarily in that dreadful dying of Jesus on a cross, in anguish and desolation, in tortures of mind and body, and that the manifest power and the miracles of God can only be understood rightly from this viewpoint.

It is a bit different with Luke. He certainly does not doubt that there are no limits to God's power and that this may become manifest in miracles. There are times in which faith will experience God in such a way. He knows at the same time that miracles also happen outside of the church (Acts 8:9–11, cf. Luke 11:19), and we have seen that he points even more frequently than Mark to the crucifixion as the goal of the whole journey of Jesus. Yet his emphasis is different from that of Mark. It lies on the true humanity of Jesus. This shows, first, in Jesus' total openness to all people, especially to women and to tax collectors, which is stressed in the Third Gospel more than in any of the others or even in the epistles. One has to remember what the status of a woman was in a society in which she had not even the right of witnessing in court, and in which men prayed: "I thank thee that thou hast not created me . . . as a woman." Neither was the tax collector an accepted or even a sympathetic figure. As a rule, he was a wealthy and unscrupulous businessman, forced to be so by the Roman system of leasing the tax office to the one who offered the highest sum. This was so much so that one even erected a monument "to X.Y. who collected the tax so well." It is, by the way, not clear whether he did it well with regard to the taxpayers or to the government; we only are told that he emigrated later to what today is Switzerland and founded there a bank, which implies that he certainly must have done well for himself.[53] More important is the fact that Luke portrays Jesus' life in a way which brings it as close to the lives of other people as possible. His coming into the world and even his later destiny is, according to Luke, certainly superior to that of his forerunner John the Baptist, and yet very similar to it. His whole ministry is painted as being a service for others, the basis of all serving in his church, and yet, just because of this, resembling it. His passion is, no doubt, the pivotal point of history and therefore vindicated by God raising him from the dead. Yet, in some way, it is to be re-experienced by his followers, by Stephen or by Paul, as we have seen.

What Luke conveys to his readers comes rather close to that early Christian hymn in Philippians 2:6–8: The one who was equal with God emptied himself and took the character of a slave, coming in a human likeness. The real miracle of God is just this lowness of the life and death of Jesus. It consists of the fact that he, God, is able to achieve what a person cannot achieve. An individual can be great, occasionally, in the most propitious hours of history. One may compose a symphony, write a poem, paint a picture, or perform an extreme act of love by which generations are stimulated, comforted, enchanted. But one cannot be truly low without resistance, conscious or unconscious, against one's destiny, without accumulating more and more opposition in one's unconscious self until it breaks out with a vengeance, even if one succeeded in swallowing the bitter pill first. God performed the miracle of all miracles. He became truly low, still remaining God in his unlimited power, even being God in exactly this way. Luke knows, in a very concrete, even "pictorial" way that in Jesus God became truly man, but as God had intended in creation. In this sense Jesus is the only true man. The ancient formula "truly God and truly [human]" expresses the truth that God is God exactly in his being truly human. It is quite clear to Luke that wherever one succeeds to lead a truly human life, it is pre-experience or a re-experience of what the life and death of Jesus was. Therefore this formula most certainly does not say that the person, or the person in his or her best parts is God. It says that the miracle has happened that God encountered the world in a truly human life and death, and that this gives meaning and sense to all the fragmentary achievements of true humanity in history as they are illustrated in the history of Israel and of the church.

3. Luke's parable of the powerless omnipotent

This parable is a piece of Lukan tradition which became for me in the last decade the key text for the understanding of who God is. It is certainly a pre-Lukan parable, very probably an authentic parable of Jesus himself. We usually call it the Parable of the Prodigal Son, which is undoubtedly wrong, since this title covers only the first part of the story. It begins with the words "a man" describing the father, and it ends with a saying of the father (15:11, 31–32). Moreover, all the unexpected acts are acts of the father, whereas the two sons act, by and large, as we should expect them to act. Thus the father is clearly the central figure which is present through the whole story. Without claiming to scoop out all that is to be found in this parable, it seems to me wise to concentrate on the father. If there ever was a permissive, even anti-authoritarian father, it is the father of Jesus' story. He simply hands over to the younger son the full amount of what he will inherit, in one fit of generosity, though he must know what his son will do with it. Is he an "almighty" father? Of course, he is; he can do whatever he wants to. He can say: "My son, in the time of my youth, we waited until the father was buried for good, and you will do exactly as I had to do." He can say: "Well, maybe I should raise your pocket money a bit, say a fiver more from next week on." He can say: "We might discuss whether you should have the interest of what will belong to you after my death." He can say a hundred more things and propose any solution that he likes, and he can act and see to it that it will be done precisely as he suggested it. And yet he is a totally powerless father, because he knows that he will lose his son if he does oppose him now. The almighty father has become powerless because he has decided to love his son. Therefore there is but one road to go. He has to let his son go and even help him to sever from his father.

We know how the story proceeds. It happens as the father could have foreseen. The son goes to seed in that foreign city, far away from his real home. The father is still something like an almighty father. He could go fetch his son in the city and bring him back. He could send a friend to do so. He might perhaps even phone Interpol and get the police on the job, and they would find the son and bring him back where he belongs. But again, he is actually totally powerless. If he acted in this way he would without any doubt lose his son forever. There is again only one road to go. He has to wait without using any of his power, wait with a heart burning of love in which he accompanies from far away his son on his travels. It is the decision to love him that renders him powerless. We know how the son returns, how the father sees him when he is still far away, because the father has constantly waited for him, always having been on the lookout for him, actually never separated from him. He even cuts the son's confession short and brings him into the hall to celebrate his homecoming with that fatted calf, old wine, and dances. This looks much more like the picture that we think Jesus should have painted of his father in heaven. The father sits at the head of the table, distributing food and drink, granting fellowship and a feeling of jubilation to his son at his right hand and to all the servants around the table. But there are no snapshots we can take of God in order to put them into our picture books so that we always should know who God is and what he looks like. God is a living God, and therefore it would, at least, have to be a movie and even a never-ending movie which would give us a kind of picture of him.

That gorgeous picture of father and son and all the servants united at the banquet is not the end of the parable. The real shock comes in the last verses of the story. The elder son stands outside and refuses to join the company of the festival group at the family table. And where is the father? He is not in the banquet hall. There is only the good-for-nothing younger son. The father is out in the darkness where his rebelling son looks back in anger to what he has achieved and what the father has given him. Is the father still the almighty father? Yes. He could call some of his servants and they would get the son into the hall within five minutes. And yet he is totally powerless because he has decided to love his elder son as he had loved his younger one. Therefore the story of Jesus ends with the younger son enjoying food and drink and dancing, and the powerless almighty father out in the darkness where he could catch pneumonia, having nothing but a heart full of love and his word that invites the elder son to join him and his brother in deep joy. This end of the story grips the hearts of the hearers, because there is no solution given. Jesus leaves us with the picture of the powerless father out there. And over against him stands that righteous elder son who is so thoroughly convinced that, if there were an almighty father, he would have to act in a quite different way. This is the figure which comes towards the hearer of the parable and asks whether it is not the hearer who is standing there.

To say the same in modern terminology,[54] it is the Oedipus situation which is described in this parable. The younger son wants to get rid of his father, to "kill" him. He desires to be himself without a dominant father figure behind him. So he goes to a "far country" and squanders himself. But he needs a substitute for the father, a "citizen of that country." Because this is a very hard father, the escape of the younger son has failed. Now he has to go back to his real father, but no longer as his son. He will now be his slave, a mere object, a piece of property. It is not so very different with the elder son. He identifies himself with his father, but with his father as he should be in his own view. In this way he also gets rid of him and "kills" the real father. But his father comes after him, and it seems that he still will dominate him and force him to subjection. Thus it looks as though the only solution would be to stay in an infantile status, to subject oneself totally to the will and the power of the father.

The most surprising fact of this story is the attitude of this father who does not want to dominate, to subject his sons to his own will. The story of the two sons seems to run down to the end in a well-known psychological pattern. But in the parable of Jesus, the father butts in. He does not want to possess his sons. In an incredible way he leads them to total freedom, which the younger son finds in the home of the father and which the elder son also should find there. The father does not even preach a sermon or wait for a confession of sins. On the contrary, he cuts it short in the case of the younger son, and he accepts his elder one without reserve: "Son, you are always with me and all that is mine is yours." There is no word to the younger son, only the act of welcome, and there is but a word of affirmation to the elder one. What this father demonstrates with his acts is rather more like a sacramental manifestation of an incredible love than like preaching.

Jesus has not merely told this parable. He has lived it. Perhaps only a month or two later he is hanging on the cross, people shouting at him: "Descend from the cross, and we shall believe in you." Is this the almighty God? Jesus could have prayed, and his father would have sent him more than twelve legions of angels (Matt. 26:53). And yet he is totally powerless, because he has decided to love. Therefore he has nothing, not even a square inch of land to stay upon, not even the freedom to move his hand or foot an inch to the left or to the right. Nailed securely on solid wood, separated from the earth on which he was living, he is hanging there in total powerlessness. He has nothing more than his heart full of love and a few last words by which he invites the people around him to join him and to come to the banquet hall of the father.

It is Jesus who has told *and* lived the parable of the powerless almighty father, Jesus who knows his father in heaven better than anyone else knows him. Should it not be true that this his father in heaven is to be found, first of all, where the father stands at the end of the parable—out in the dark where the rebels are fighting against him? The New Testament says that he is to be found on the cross, and this means there where his limitless love is waiting and suffering and inviting until all people return—not forced, not even persuaded, but out of a heart that has been really moved—to the one who loves them. If this is true, if God is similar to the father of Jesus' parable, then the burning questions about, for instance, why God could let that dreadful holocaust of Jews happen and could not let the attacks on the life of Hitler succeed are not solved. Instead, they are taken up in a way that lets them look differently. The God of the debate between atheists and believers, the God whom some want to prove and others to disprove is a powerful, almighty lord who rules over all. The God of the New Testament is, first of all, the powerless man nailed to the cross, and only when we have found God there shall we also experience his power of loving and helping, his real omnipotence.

4. Jesus—Christ, Son of God, Servant of the Lord

Up to now we have seen what the authors of the New Testament and what Jesus himself told us about God's coming into the world. What does Jesus teach about himself? There is the surprising fact that Jesus never called himself "the messiah." The word "Christ" (in Hebrew: the messiah, "the annointed one") appears more than 500 times in the New Testament. It was never used by Jesus himself,[55] whereas the title Son of man is used, with the exception of Acts 7:56, exclusively in sayings of Jesus himself. I think that the report of the confession of Peter is basically correct and that he called Jesus the messiah. According to Mark 8:30 Jesus neither rejected nor accepted that title, but rebuked his disciples (as he rebuked the demon in 1:25) and charged them not to tell anyone about him.[56] He threw the switch immediately to another track, speaking about the Son of man who is to suffer and to be rejected. Whether the high priest used the term "Christ" or not is historically uncertain because no one of the disciples was present at that trial, and it is not easy to imagine one of the members of the court having told the details of this hearing to the disciples of Jesus. If the report is correct and if Jesus has accepted that title unambiguously (which he has according to Mark 14:62, but not according to Matt. 26:64 and Luke 22:70), the situation of the defendant to be condemned to death within the next hour interprets that title in a totally new way. Be this as it may, it remains true that Jesus himself did not use the title, but at most accepted it when uttered by others.

Yet there is no doubt about the fact that Jesus called people to follow him. This is surprisingly new. The Jewish rabbi does not call disciples; the young man who wants to become his disciple asks him whether he would be permitted to follow him. His teacher leads him to the text of the Scriptures and to a detailed interpretation of the Word of God as it was spoken centuries ago. The disciple who follows Jesus does not expect to be led into an auditorium where he learns the rules of interpretation of ancient texts. He is taken on a journey by his master, and nobody knows where it will lead. But more than any rabbi, Jesus urges him to follow him and seems to imply that his life or even his eternal life may depend on his decision whether or not to comply with that demand. The main difference is still another: The disciple who follows the rabbi hopes to become a rabbi himself, as good or even better than his master, if God will grant him this. No disciple of Jesus ever dreamed of becoming a Son of man himself. This concept of following Jesus was so unique that even the post-Easter church never used the word of its obedience to the risen Lord, except in Revelation 14:4. Following Jesus is restricted to the time of the earthly Jesus, though the stories about the disciples following him certainly challenged and invited the readers of the Gospels to do something very similar in their different situation.

It is also true that Jesus did forgive sins. Even if none of the words that speak expressly of it are authentic, Jesus doubtless acted with such forgiveness. Otherwise all the reports of table fellowship with publicans, of allowing a prostitute to anoint him during a festival meal in a wholly male company, of being together with all sorts of questionable people, often without visible success of converting them, would not be thinkable. Even more in favor of authenticity are the reactions that this behavior of Jesus stirred up (cf. Matt. 11:19, etc.). Forgiving of sins, however, is the exclusive privilege of God himself, as the opponents of Jesus state correctly (Mark 2:7). The formula ". . . but I say to you" (with an emphasized "I") may be debated with regard to its authenticity—though I myself consider it authentic—but Jesus' call to love the enemies and his new interpretation of what "do not kill" or "do not commit adultery" means are not to be doubted. If the saying against a letter of divorce is authentic (which is probably so), his new interpretation even contradicted a Mosaic law explicitly. When acting so (as is true of all his teaching), Jesus never used the introductory formula of the prophets ("Thus speaks the Lord") which points away from the speaker to another source of the word. Neither did he use the formula of the teacher of the law ("Thus it is written in . . ."). He starts his sayings, "Truly, I say to you . . . ." Finally, the whole development of the Jesus movement in the early church with charismatic healings, prophecies, and new tongues would become inexplicable if much of this were not already alive in the ministry of Jesus. He certainly healed people, whether in a psychologically explicable way or not, and he certainly preached with a remarkable authority in which God's presence in the living word (which was considered as having discontinued after the death of the last great prophet) became alive again.[57]

Even as historians who read their sources in a very critical approach, we could not but say that, in the view of the material that we possess, the picture of a harmless Jesus is out of the question. This man was either totally crazy—from religious mania or superdeveloped self-estimation—or he was what he claimed to be, the one in whom God himself encounters the world in a totally unique way. Either—or. There is no other choice. But if we choose the latter alternative, we face the surprising fact that, though Jesus acted and preached in a way which excelled everything people had expected of the messiah, he never claimed explicitly to be the messiah. Why?

Equally sure is the fact that Jesus never used the term "Son of God" when speaking of himself. The title is missing in the first three Gospels, as far as Jesus' own sayings are concerned. It may be that the chief priest used it (Mark 14:61), or the bystanders (Luke 22:70), and that Jesus accepted it, though this is very uncertain. Jesus may, however, have spoken about "the father" and "the son" (Mark 13:32 and Matt. 11:27). This is not exactly the same. When we say "Son of God" we stress his superiority over sons of human parents. When Jesus puts "the son" over against "the father," he emphasizes the dependence of the son on the father and the superiority of the father. (This, at least, was true for his time and the understanding of his generation, though our youngsters may think differently today.) Even if these words are authentic, which is not beyond all doubt, Jesus did not use the title in a formal way. If he spoke of "the son" (of the one "father," God), he did not stress the superiority of this son over all other persons, but the superiority of God over the son.

And again, not speaking of the Son of God, Jesus *acted* as the Son of God. This is true for the sayings just mentioned above, if they are his own words. Both express his unity with and his dependence on his father: "Of that day or that hour nobody knows, not even the angels in heaven nor the son, but only the father," and "No one knows the son except the father . . . ." Be these words authentic

or not, Jesus certainly lived in an awareness of his specific relation
to his father in heaven, which was something quite different from
that of other people. In our whole tradition we never find the phrase
"our father" which would connect Jesus and the disciples. This is
because the Lord's Prayer is, according to Luke 11:2, addressed
simply to the "father" and, according to Matthew 6:9, given to the
disciples who should pray "our father" (with an emphasized "you
[shall pray]"). Admittedly, the evidence is not very clear, since there
is in Mark but one example of "your father" and, in Q, conversely,
but one of "my father" (Luke 10:22, where reading is not beyond all
doubts). Nonetheless, the negative evidence is clear: There is never
an "our father" which sees Jesus in the same relation to God as the
disciples. The term "abba" is to be found only in Mark 14:36, but
the hypothesis that it was introduced from a liturgical usage in the
early church (cf. Rom. 8:15; Gal. 4:6) is certainly not very convincing, especially when seen in the light of the synoptic evidence which
shows that almost all the prayers of Jesus are addressed exclusively
to the "father." This was unique in Palestine in the time of Jesus. If
"father" appears at all in the address only after the time of Jesus,
(as far as our evidence goes), it is connected with the title "king."
The term does appear within the prayer but rarely, and this is different, because it comes close to a simile when one prays, for instance;
"Thou art our father who cares for us."[58] Thus again, there is no
harmless Jesus. He did not use "Son of God" as a title, but he lived
and spoke and acted as the one who thought of being in a unique
relation to his father in heaven. Again this was either extreme in-
sanity or the truth, because he was the one to whom God was father
in an exclusive way.

Something very similar is to be said about the title "Servant of
God." No Gospel or any other New Testament writing reports that
Jesus had ever used this term. There is but one section in which it is
mentioned, Acts 3 and 4. Even here, it is not clear at all what it
means, because Acts 3:13, 26 use it in a context suggesting Isaiah
53, though stressing glorification more than delivery of the servant,
whereas Acts 4:25, 30 see the term as equivalent with "Lord" and
"Christ" (vs. 26), in the same sense as David the King was servant
of God. Outside of Acts 3 and 4 we find only one Old Testament

quotation in which "my servant" is mentioned (Matt. 12:18), even
there in no way connected with the suffering or the death of Jesus,
but rather with healings that he performed.

Again, this does not mean that Jesus' ministry was not influenced or even imprinted by Deutero-Isaiac passages about
the servant of the Lord, though it is difficult to be sure. Be this
as it may, he suffered, not merely like the servant of God in
Isaiah 53, but in a way which went far beyond anything anyone
could have imagined in connection with the coming of the suffering servant. He did not die in the way Judaism of that time
expected the suffering righteous to die. He did not die sur-
rounded by his friends and followers, his group mates, accom-
panying him in intercession and admiration. Nor did he die in
a kind of trance in which he was so much in union with God
that he did not feel any of the sufferings and pains. He died in
desolation, relinquished, betrayed, denied by his own disciples
and seeing that not only he himself but also his cause was lost.
Admittedly, Luke smooths this picture in some ways, describing
Jesus rather as a kind of exemplary martyr, praying for his enemies, caring for the criminals crucified with him and open to
God into whose hands he commends his soul. As we have seen,
Luke is very much interested in an understanding of the suffering of Jesus as something which could be re-experienced, so
that it is infinitely more than an idea which one could simply
take over intellectually or even emotionally without getting involved in his total life. He certainly emphasizes no less than the
other synoptists that Jesus lived and died in a way which surpassed by far anything that was connected with the destiny of
the Servant of the Lord, as Judaism of that time saw it.

Thus again the historian is forced to state that this is no harmless Jesus. Either he was a masochist with a strong religious background longing for and in some way perhaps even enjoying his suffering, or he was the Servant of the Lord, indeed, who in his
crucifixion fulfilled the will of God.

5. Jesus, Son of man

There seems to be just, perhaps decisive, exception to what

we have seen up to now. Did Jesus not use the title of Son of man when speaking of himself? This is one of the most debated problems of New Testament interpretation, and it is just impossible to deal with it thoroughly here.[59] If I see correctly, there are three or four main approaches to a solution. First, some scholars think that Son of man was actually a title describing the heavenly figure of the one who would come at the end of the world as judge and savior, as depicted in IV Ezra 13 and Ethiopic Enoch's similitudes. Therefore they conclude that the title was not used by Jesus himself but only by the post-Easter church. It is to be found only in sayings of Jesus, because the usage of this title was restricted to Christian prophets who used to speak in the name of the risen Lord and therefore in the first person singular, thus creating new sayings of Jesus. The difficulty of this approach is, on the one hand, the date of the sources. IV Ezra was written after the destruction of Jerusalem (70 A.D.). The similitudes of Ethiopic Enoch may have been written, in the Aramaic or Hebrew original, as late as the second century A.D. and what we possess is a translation of a translation of an original text.[60] On the other hand there are statistics, as mentioned earlier: the title *Christ* over 500 times outside of the sayings of Jesus, and almost never in them; *Son of man* once outside of them, otherwise only in the mouth of Jesus. Even if it had been a favorite title of prophets, would it never have entered the language of the church about Jesus, though it had originated in that same church?

Second, some scholars think that Jesus used the title, but expected another Son of man coming at the end of the world. He would be a figure related to Jesus but not identical with him, judging people according to their attitude towards Jesus. This is, in my view, the most improbable suggestion. Would Jesus ever have used a title known only in some esoteric apocalyptic groups while avoiding current titles like messiah or Son of God or even Servant of the Lord or prophet, titles that would be very open to different interpretations? Moreover, if Jesus had expected still another one, could he have acted in a way which seemed to indicate that his teaching, his healing, his living and dying went far beyond what people had expected the messiah, the Son of God or the Servant of the Lord to do? And if so, why did the church not go on expecting this other

Son of man? The resurrection of Jesus would just prove that he was right, that he was the true prophet vindicated by God himself and that, therefore, this other Son of man would surely come. Third, other scholars thought that the Son of man concept was not more than a vague idea forming the background of very different inter-pretations, some even using the term as a corporate title of the mes-sianic congregation. Daniel 7:13, the key passage that speaks of the Son of man, could have been applied—perhaps even in this se-quence—to the exaltation or ascension, to the crucifixion and to the parousia of Jesus. The main problem of this solution is the same as that of the first one. If this application to Jesus was mainly or exclu-sively given by the early church why does it not appear outside of the sayings of the earthly Jesus?

Fourth, I personally think that Jesus used the term when speaking of himself, just because it was not a title nor merely a vague idea. Other scholars propose similar solutions in the same direction. Since "Son of man" means in Aramaic not more than "man" (as an individual, not in the sense of a generic designa-tion), Jesus may have used it as a kind of challenge to his hear-ers: Does he just speak of himself as a man like any other or does he use this circumlocution because he wants to point to something special? In this sense, I think, Jesus spoke of the "Son of man" who has nowhere to lay his head (Matt. 8:20), or of the "Son of man" of whom people say that he is a glutton and a drunkard (Matt. 11:19). In the same sense he would tell his dis-ciples that the Son of man would have to be rejected and to suf-fer (which is, in my view, the authentic core of Mark 8:31) or to be "delivered into the hands of men" (Mark 9:31). In the same sense, Jesus finally expected his vindication by God, which means that he would be exalted to God and appear as the key witness in the last judgment, just as Jews before Jesus had ex-pected it of the suffering righteous who calls himself servant of God and God his father, who is tortured and put to a shameful death, but will appear among the angels of God to his oppo-nents (probably in the last judgment), witnessing against them (Wisd. 2:12–20; 5:1–5). This is what Luke 12:8 and other passages express. That the chief witness in God's last judgment was seen more and more as the judge himself is quite natural and understandable, since the verdict actually depends only on his testimony. In 1 Corinthians 4:4–5 the same sentence contains the concept of Jesus being the judge and of God being the judge; 2 Corinthians 5:10 mentions the judgment seat of Christ just as Romans 14:10 mentions the one of God. Whether the usage of the term in Daniel 7:13 or the frequent addresses of Ezekiel as Son of man by God were more central for Jesus can be left open. At any rate, this would explain why Son of man appears only in the sayings of Jesus, but covers his earthly ministry as well as his suffering and dying and his decisive role in the last judgment. The difficulty of this solution is the combination of two different background motives, that of the (apocalyptic) Son of man and that of the (sapiential) suffering righteous.

I do not think that it is possible to decide which of these or what other solution is the true one, as long as we do not find new evidence of Jewish or Christian references to this term.[61] However, it seems highly probable that Son of man was a title which would define Jesus in a rather definite way and that, in this case, it was not taken up by him, just because it was more of a riddle or a simile than a definition of who he actually was.

6. The experience of God cannot be taught: Luke's challenge to theology, Christology, and pneumatology

So we are back to what I tried to say earlier. Jesus refuses to give us a title which defines him and which we just could carry home in order to know who he is. It seems to be of first importance to him that people could approach him in a very open way without knowing beforehand who he is. Therefore he spoke in parables rather than in dogmatic statements. Therefore it is only the church after Easter that had to find its own words to proclaim him that may have said: "Now, this Jesus of Nazareth, he is really the messiah," because "messiah" was now defined by all the experiences which the disciples had made in following Jesus during his ministry, his arrest and death, and in the appearances of the risen Lord. This is the crucial point. Mathematics can be taught. I know that I shall succeed in conveying at least a basic mathematic knowledge to the students of my class if they are not totally incapable of development. Perhaps this year I need a double amount of time compared with last year, but the goal is certainly reachable. But the experience of God cannot be taught. In this respect, he is closer to the phenomena of music or painting, or even more, of love. The experience of music, painting, and especially, of love cannot be taught. I can certainly help somebody to have these experiences. I can take my son to the art museum, and, pointing to this or to that when going with him along a wall full of pictures, I may succeed in starting a process in him. This may lead him to ever new discoveries and experiences. But I cannot convey these experiences directly. He cannot simply listen to my explications, accept them, reflect upon them, and then possess them as his own understanding. Whether it happens that he learns to understand music or painting or even love is always dependent on the question of whether I could start a process which goes on independently of my teaching, whether I could start in him a movement in which a symphony, a school of painters, or an experience of genuine love comes to life. I can, at best, open him to what these experiences themselves have to teach him. If music, painting, or love cannot be taught, certainly the experience of God cannot be taught. Teaching is very important to help individuals towards that experience in which they will be moved by an encounter with music, painting, love, or even God. But teaching cannot convey real knowledge, because there is no guarantee that it will lead to that encounter.

We have asked: "Who is Jesus Christ?" The New Testament tells us that God is not that almighty, eternal, highest being, detached from all the suffering and all the problems of the world. It tells us that, on the contrary, God is to be found where we see nothing but powerlessness, even total surrender to those who rebel against him, and that this becomes manifest in the crucified man nailed to a cross, not able to move his hands or feet, no longer standing on firm soil. It is a Lukan parable which depicts that father who was not sitting in the banquet hall in heavenly jubilation and authority, but waiting outside on a chilly and dark evening pleading with a rebelling son. If we take this seriously, if we learn to confess that truth of God to be found in Jesus, even in a crucified Jesus, then we stop dreaming of a God of whom we would possess a fixed picture as valid for ever. To search for a definition of God would be as silly as getting just one snapshot of the father sitting at the head of the table in the midst of abundant food and drink and music and dance and thinking that this were all that we had to know about him. To be sure, this also is the father, but if we think that we know now who he is, we will not recognize him ten minutes later. Though this picture is a live photograph, and not completely wrong, we can never substitute it for the parable of Jesus because it is only true in the context of what the parable tells us of this father before and after the festival meal. The snapshot would only be true if it would also show the heart of the father which went with his younger son through all the troubles and fears and shameful defeats of his journey in the foreign land, and which moves him to go after his elder son. If we know that, we shall not think that there is a ready-to-wear Jesus whom the theological teacher could just hand over to us, neatly wrapped in so many sentences, to be carried home like the suit we bought, wrapped in tissue paper and plastic bag by the shop assistant. When we say that God is to be found in Jesus, this statement implies that he is to be found where Jesus comes alive today, and that we never know in advance where and how this will happen. It goes without saying that we shall not encounter another Jesus than the one the New Testament witnesses tell us about. But as Jesus dismisses the hearers of his parables with the call, "He who has ears to hear let him hear," so all the witnesses of the New Testament try to set some process in motion in which we shall meet the one they have met. Never can we get hold of Jesus by just getting hold of some sentences that describe him. It will always be the living Jesus who will speak through the words of those who witness to him.

This is exactly what we have found in Luke. He is very reluctant to give us any clear Christological statements or titles. Neither are there definite patterns of God's nature or of his role in history. Luke certainly says that God can use and does use history to manifest himself, but there are no rules that we could handle to detect his acts or even to predict them.

Nor is there a definite pneumatology in Luke. How confusing are the reports in Acts! Once the Spirit is given without baptism

(2:4), often immediately after or in baptism (2:38, etc.), once also before (10:44) and twice quite a time after baptism (8:16–17; 19:6). Moreover, the Spirit once given to someone has still to come anew (for instance, 4:31). There is no doctrine of the Spirit which would shield us against ever-new surprises by the living God, of whose love we know, but not how he will act on us. This is why Luke tells so many stories. They are not stories in which some general and timeless truth could be conveyed to the hearer but are, in the understanding of Luke, definitely reports of what has happened in history. He may shift, for instance, the story of the first preaching of Jesus in Nazareth to another place, or he may, perhaps, prefer this tradition to the other one in Mark. This shows that he does not consider important the details of when and where and how exactly it happened. The story would become void if it did not express what had happened in the life and death and resurrection of Jesus. And yet it would be impossible to select just one or a few of these stories thinking that this would be the definite picture of who Jesus is. It may be this story today or that one tomorrow, or this for me and that for another person which tells us who Jesus really is. Without an openness for God's coming through these stories or these reports of Jesus' teaching—an openness which never ends—we shall not find God in them.[62]

7. The situation today

This means that we should listen seriously to a younger generation that is no longer interested in our statements and dogmas and Christological titles. It is a generation that asks where this Jesus becomes reality. I think we should earnestly hear that and let it become the first question. The people of the younger generation may hope to find this reality of a living Jesus in a social engagement for underprivileged people, or in an individual experience of meditation, or in a charismatically moved group and its different gifts. Perhaps it is not of first importance whether it is here or there. Just because they have no fixed image of who Jesus is, they are able to let themselves be surprised by him. Just because they are open for an encounter which might happen in a totally unorthodox way, they may have an advantage over us. They know that all the correct statements become wrong if they do not become living reality, and we should gratefully learn that from them.

Certainly this is not the last word to be said. The genuine, un-prejudiced encounter with the living Jesus is always only the beginning of a long journey, in the same way as the call to the disciples to follow him was such a beginning. They had, at that time, no idea as to what this call would imply. They did not possess any Christology or soteriology related to that call. They did not even know whether they would go with Jesus for a few hours, for a few days, for a few weeks, or even longer than that. They had to learn all this by being and living with him. They were helped, first of all, by himself in this process of learning, but they also got help from one another. The longer they walked with him, the better they learned to understand how much they depended on his ever-renewed help and how little they really understood who he was, but also how much they needed the team of those who followed him as they did. They realized this best when they were at the end of their tether, when their enthusiasm died down and their engagement was close to zero, as for instance in the Garden of Gethsemane. The pivotal point was just the day on which all their Jesus experiences broke down, on which they desperately needed the new message which the risen Lord brought then.

Thus it is just when we are at the end of all our individual experiences that we realize what the team of disciples, the body of Christ, the church means. One of the most important contributions that Luke made to the New Testament is that he certainly often speaks of individual experiences, of joy and challenge, guidance and warning, comfort and help granted to an individual disciple, and he always sees this in the context of the church. This is where we detect the importance of dogmatic formulae and of confessional creeds. We cannot do without our fellow disciples and their experiences throughout the centuries, from the New Testament times to ours. These experiences of others who may have understood Jesus better than we ourselves are handed down in the books of the New Testament, presupposing the experiences of which the Old Testament tells and without which the New Testament testimony would become wrong. They are

also handed down in the credal formulae or the confessions of
the church, in the books and the reports of the lives of so many
Christians, and we could not live in faith without them. We
would understand them wrongly if we tried to take them over
like mathematical theorems. We understand them rightly if we
realize that they are a help to set us anew in motion towards a
new encounter with Jesus himself, to draw us back from going
astray or to save us from getting stubborn in our fixed ideas.
Just being convinced that confession formulae can never capture
God, teach the experience of God, or manage him can open us
to the truth that the church can never live without them. We
need them so desperately just because we do not possess Jesus
forever in our individual experiences and picture of him. It is
even possible and sometimes urgent that the church keep some
confessional statements without understanding them, as a re-
minder of some truth that it is unable to see now, but will need
urgently in another situation. By and large the Hellenistic
church of the second and third centuries did not understand eschatology. It was too much tied up with the Greek idea of time
as an endless circular movement, ever repeating itself, to be able
to preach eschatology in a meaningful way. It kept the credal
formula of the one to come to judge the quick and the dead in
its liturgy, and suddenly, with Augustine, this came to life again
and became of first importance for the further development of
the church. Thus we have to remember what I said earlier: In
some respects, Paul is more important than Luke for the church.
In times of uncertainty, of temptation to go on wrong roads, of
attacks by those who fight against God, it is of first importance
to know about unambiguously clear directions. But, in other respects, it is the wealth of stories about Jesus and his work in the
church provided by Luke's Gospel and Acts which is of first importance, just because it is impossible to misunderstand it as a
final definition of who Jesus Christ and, therefore, who God is.
A correct theology, Christology, and pneumatology are never the
road itself on which to drive, but they are the barriers that stop
us from getting lost or even killing ourselves. The stories of Luke
and Acts are certainly not the road either, but they show us

what the road looks like so that we can detect it when we come to it and distinguish it from the surrounding swamps or sands. Thus they may become the receptacle in which the living Jesus Christ is brought to us.

Who is Jesus Christ? If we answer, with the old confession formula, that he is truly God and truly human, or that he is the Son of the Father from eternity to eternity, then we express something of the event character of God. By saying so we state that God is not that most high secluded being, of whom we dream. He is not simply the absolute ideal of what we experience and know in our world. By saying so we state, on the contrary, that God is a living God but a God who was and is and will be moving. God is the movement of love, love from the Father to the Son and from the Son back to the Father and as the Spirit radiating into creation, long before there was any world outside of him and forever after this world will have ceased to be. This certainly means that he is also the power of all genuine love in our world. It does not say, however, that love, as we may experience it in individual charity or social involvement, is God, but it does say that such love is always emanating from the one love that is living God from eternity. The question "Who is Jesus Christ?"—and therefore also the question "Who is God?"—will be answered only by those who are as open to their contemporaries who question the reality of their statements as they are to their fathers and brothers and mothers and sisters in the body of Christ of all ages and their questions and answers.

Notes

1 For the following, cf. Eduard Schweizer, "Neues Testament and Verkundigung," *Biblische Studien* 56, Neukirchen-Vluyn, 1969, 9–23.

2 I have tried to show that in my essay "Resurrection–Fact or Illusion?" in *Horizons in Biblical Theology* I, Pittsburgh, 1979, 137–159, on pp. 145–149.

3 A. von Harnack, *Das Wesen des Christentums*, Leipzig, 1962, 52; Chr. Blumhardt, *Predigten und Andachten,* ed. R. Lejeune, I - V, Erlenbach/Zurich, 1925f; L. Ragaz, *Gedanken aus vierzig Jahren geistigen Kampfes,* Bern, 1951 (second edition, with full bibliography), also idem, *Mein Weg,* Zurich, 1952.

4 *The Quest of the Historical Jesus,* London, 1932, 331–332.

5 *Der Romerbrief,* Munich, 1922, (6, also V) (preface to the first ed., 1918, XIII) (to the second ed.), p. 324f.; idem, *Kirchliche Dogmatik* I/1, Munich, 1932, 146; idem, *Theologische Existenz heute* 1, Munich, 1933, 11–13, 40; ibid. no. 9, 1934, 15–23.

6 Cf. K. Barth, *Romerbrief* (note 5) XIX (preface to the third ed.).

7 *Theologie des Neuen Testaments,* preliminary remarks, pp. 1–2; also 7, 1, p. 45.

8 *Exegetica,* Tübingen, 1967, 469; idem, *Neues Testament und Mythologie,* in *Offenbarung und Heilsgescheben,* Munich, 1941, 63–67 (= *Kerygma and Mythos,* Hamburg, 1948, 47–51).

9 P. Stuhlmacher, *Schriftauslegung,* Göttingen, 1975: *Neues Testament und Hermeneutik* (originally in *ZThK* 68, 1971, 121–161) Ch. V, pp. 24–31.

10 "Die Problematik einer Theologie des Neuen Testamentes," in *Gesammelte Studien zum Neuen Testament und seiner Umwelt,* Tübingen, 2nd ed. 1967, 341; idem, "Gottes Existenz und meine Geschichtlichkeit im Neuen Testament," in *Zeit und Geschichte,* R. Bultmann, 1964, 418–421; idem, *Jesus,* Stuttgart, 1969, 71, 159–170.

11 *Die Auferstehung Jesu als historisches und als theologisches Problem,* Gutersloh, 1964, 25–26; idem, *Die Auferstehung Jesu von Nazareth,* Gutersloh, 1968, 144, 150–151, also 18–27

12 "Das Problem des historischen Jesus," *ZThK* 51, 1954, 125–153; idem, "Die Anfange christlicher Theologie," *ZThK* 57, 1960, 162–185 (=idem, *Exegetische Versuche und Besinnungen* I, Göttingen, 1960, 187–214, esp. 212–214; II, 1968, 82–104, esp. 100; I rather suggested "midwife" instead of "mother," in *Jesus und Paulus*, W.G. Kummel, Göttingen, 1975, 314). Cf. Gisel (next note) 594, 649: history as text of the theology.

13 *Verite et histoire*, Paris/Geneva, 1977; esp. 37–38, 581–653.

14 *Resurrection de Jesus et message pascal*, Paris, 1971, esp. 291, 305.

15 *Theologie des Alten Testamentes* II, Munich, 1960, 370–371, cf. W. Zimmerli, ibid. 348.

16 In *Offenbarung als Geschichte*, Göttingen, 1961, esp. 98–106, 393–413; idem, *Grundzuge er Christologie*, Gutersloh, 1964.

17 H.-P. Hasenfratz, *Die Rede von der Auferstehung Jesu Christi*, Bonn, 1975, 37–50, esp. 38, 206–212.

18 *Existiert Gott?* Munich, 1978, 127, also 128–133, 487–488; cf. idem, *Christ sein*, Munich, 1974, for instance pp. 55–61, 506.

19 *Dogmatik des christlichen Glaubens* I-III, Tübingen, 1979, esp. I 297–304.

20 *Grundkurs des Glaubens*, Freiburg, 1976, 143–202 (esp. 176f., 200–202).

21 *Jesus*, Freiburg, 1975; idem, *Christus und die Christen*, Freiburg, 1977 (esp. 25–69).

22 *Der gekreuzigte God*, 2nd ed. Munich, 1973, for instance 49–55, 189–192, 202–204, 220–221.

23 *Gott als Geheimnis der Welt*, 2nd ed., Tübingen, 1977, esp. 248–306 (Moltmann [note 22] formulates "death in God" [192]; cf. Gisel [note 13] 558).

24 Tübingen, 1965.

25 Moltmann (note 22), 234. Marzsen used this sentence first on Jan. 7, 1964 (idem, *Die Sache Jesu geht weiter*, Gutersloher Taschenbucher, 112 [1976], 7 = idem).

26 For a summary cf. H. Weder, *Das Kreuz Jesu bei Paulus*, FRLANT, Göttingen, 1980, part I; cf. also I.H. Marshall, *Luke: Historian and Theologian*, Pater Noster Press, 1970, 21–37; also 111–112 for Luke's understanding of *heilsgeschichte*.

27 Dionysius of Halikarnassus (first century B.C.), quoted after
   W.F. Howard, *The Fourth Gospel in Recent Criticism and Inter-*
   pretation, London, 1931, 236. Polybius, in *Hist.* VI 4.9; 9.13;
   51.4 (cf. 57; 10.2), even sees something like a law of nature behind the movement of history in ever-repeated circles.

28 Sextus Empiricus, *Adv. Math.* I 12.254.

29 Cf. on the one hand, von Rad, Rahner, Pannenberg above (I 2
   and 3); on the other, Bultmann (I 1) and Ernst Fuchs, "Christus
   das Ende der Geschichte," *EvTh* 8, 1948/9, 447–461.

30 *Die Mitte der Zeit,* 3rd ed., Tübingen, 1960, 30. The first radical
   attack was that of Ph. Vielhauser in *EvTh* 1950/1, 1–15; English
   in *Studies in Luke-Acts,* ed. L.E. Keck/J.L. Martyn, New York,
   1966, 33–50.

31 This differs from G. Klein's interpretation, according to which
   they find their definite fulfillment only now in the church
   (*Rekonstruktion und Interpretation,* Munich, 1969, 240–243).
   This seems to be impossible, because the participle of the perfect
   describes a siuation that has been reached definitely and is still
   valid. Cf. I.H. Marshall, *The Gospel of Luke,* Grand Rapids,
   1978, 41.

32 L. Schottroff/W. Stegemann, *Jesus von Nazareth, Hoffnung der*
   Armen, Urgan-Taschenoucher T 639, Stuttgart, 1978, 89–153, especially 91–102.

33 G. Friedrich, "Luke 9:51 und die Entruckungschristologie des
   Lukas," in *Orientierung an Jesus,* J. Schmid, Freiburg, 1973, 48–
   77, especially 70–74 (reprinted in idem, *Auf das Wort Kommt es*
   an).

34 There is Mary besides Zechariah (1:11–12/27–29); the
   prophetess besides the prophet (2:25/36); the mother of a
   dead child besides a father (7:12/8:41); the two sisters besides the scribe (10:25–37/38–42); the praying widow besides the praying man (11:5–7/18:1–8); the woman healed
   on a Sabbath besides the man (13:10–17/14:1–6); the
   daughter of Abraham besides his son (13:16/19:9); the
   woman baking bread besides the sowcr (13:19/21); the
   woman who lost a coin besides the shepherd who lost his
   sheep (15:3–7/8–10); the two women besides the two men at

the parousia of Christ (17:34/35); the women witnesses besides the men (8:1/2–3 and 24:22/24, etc.).

35 Cf. J.E. Alsup, *The Post-Resurrection Appearance Stories of the
Gospel Tradition,* Calwer-Verlag, 1975, especially 144–213.

36 *The Language of the Gospel,* New York, 1964, 92, and N. Perrin's
review article, "The Parables of Jesus as Parables, as Metaphors,
and as Aesthetic Objects," *JR* 47, 1967, 340, 346. Cf. W.
Harnisch's instructive review of, especially American, contributions to this topic in *Verkundigung und Forschung 1979/1
(Beiheft EvTh),* 53–89: "Die Metapher als heuristisches Prinzip."

37 In *Parables,* New York, 1973, 13.

38 Werner Heisenberg, *Der Teil und das Ganze,* Munich, 1961, 285,
quoted after H. Weder, *Die Gleichnisse Jesu als Metaphern,*
FRLANT 120, Göttingen, 1978, 5. For the identity of methods
in natural science and in theology cf. P. Gisel, in P. Ricoeur/E.
Jüngel, *Metapher, EvTh Sondercheft,* Munich, 1974, 18–19.

39 *Language, Hermeneutic and Word of God,* New York, 1966, 179,
193–198.

40 *Die Gleichnisse Jesu,* Munich, 1970, 187 (*The Parables,* Philadelphia, 1967).

41 *Jesus and the Language of the Kingdom,* Philadelphia, 1976, 89–
193, 194–199.

42 *Disclosures in den Gleichnissen Jesu,* Frankfurt/Mainz, 1977, esp.
230–258.

43 *Paulus und Jesus,* Tübingen, 1962, esp. 87–107, 135–139, also
idem, "Metaphorische Wahrheit," in *Metapher* (n. 38) 71–122.

44 "Steilung und Funktion der Metapher in der biblischen
Sprache," ibid., esp. 54–70 (also P. Gisel on Ricoeur, ibid. 5–
23); cf. idem, *La metaphore vive,* Paris, 1975, 34–40, 97–99, 310–
321, etc.; idem in *Exegesis, Problems of Method and Exercises in
Reading* (Gen. 22 and Luke 15), ed. F. Bovon/G. Rouiller, English translation (D.G. Miller) Pittsburgh, 1978, esp. pp. 321–339
("Philosophical Hermeneutics and Biblical Hermeneutics").

45 Jüngel, *Paulus und Jesus* (note 43), 130–135.

46 Stuhlmacher (note 9), 15–17 (126–129) = E. Troeltsch, *Gesammelte Schriften* II, Tübingen, 1913, 731–733.

47 *Patr Migne* 35, 2033, using "diligere" in a context which speaks

about loving one's neighbor ("charitas") and God's love to us ("dilectio"). I owe this insight to my Zurich colleague Arthur Rich.

48 Last summarizing publication of which I know: *Papsttum als okumenische Frage,* ed. Arbeitsgemeinschaft okumenischer Universitatsinstitute, Munich/Mainz, 1979; bibliography, for instance, pp. 262–263.

49 I formulated a sentence very similar to that one in a lecture in Tübingen University eight days before Rome stripped Professor Hans Küng of his authority of teaching within the Catholic Church. He was in the audience and asked in the discussion for further explications. If I remember correctly I emphasized the character of dialogue in which the church certainly must warn most seriously one of its members who seems to go astray, but always so that it listens very carefully to the questions put to the church. I also said that it is only the continuing process of asking, answering, and listening which will finally lead to the truth which we cannot get hold of in one correct formula, even if it be a very long and detailed one.

50 For this chapter, I used parts of an essay of mine written in German: "Wer ist dieser Jesus Christus?" in *ThLZ* 99, 1974, 721–732. I have rewritten these paragraphs in the light of what I hope to have learned from the research on the Gospel of Luke, but have also tried to keep the original form of a public lecture.

51 Cf. U.B. Muller, "Die christologische Absicht des Markusevangeliums und die Verklarungsgeschichte," *ZNW* 64, 1973, 150–193; U. Luz, "Theologia crucis als Mitte der Theologie im Neuen Testament," *EvTh* 34, 1974, 131–139.

52 E. Schweizer, "Die theologische Leistung des Markus," *EvTh* 24, 1964, 337–355, reprinted in idem, *Beitrage zur Theologie des Neuen Testamentes,* Zurich, 1970, 21–42; cf. the pattern of the structure of Mark's Gospel as given in my essay, "The Portrayal of the Life of Faith in the Gospel of Mark," in *Interpretation* 32, 1978, pp. 388–389, and also N. Perrin, "Towards an Interpretation of the Gospel of Mark," in *Christology and Modern Pilgrimage,* ed. H.D. Betz, Claremont, Calif., 1971.

53 (H. L. Strack and) P. Billerbeck, *Kommentar zum Neuen Testa-*

ment aus Talmud and Midrasch III, Munich, 1961, 611; Seutonius, *Vita* 8.2.

54 Cf. L. Beirnaert, "The Parable of the Prodigal Son, Luke 15:11–32" in *Exegesis* (n. 44) 197–210.

55 Mark 9:41 formulates: "Whoever gives you a cup of water to drink because you bear the name of Christ . . . ," but the parallel in Matthew 10:42 contains the wording "in the name of a disciple" (because you are a disciple), which is certainly the more original form of the saying. This form must even have belonged to the pre-Markan tradition, because only so is the chain of links by catchwords in Mark 9:37–50 uninterrupted: "in my name" (vs. 37) is connected with "in your name" (vs. 38); "in my name" (vs. 39) to "in the name of a disciple" (vs. 41, in the form of Matt. 10:42); "one of those little ones" (same verse) to "one of those little ones" (vs. 42); "makes them stumble" (vs. 42) to the same verb in vs. 43; "fire" at the end of this saying (vs. 48) to "fire" in vs. 49; and finally "to be salted" in the same verse to "salt" in the closing verse (vs. 50). The discussion about Christ being the "Son of David" in Mark 12:35 does not directly apply that title to Jesus, but speaks in general of the figure of the messiah. Whether this is an authentic saying of Jesus is questionable. At any rate, the term "Christ" could not be avoided in a discussion of the scribal emphasis on the Davidic sonship of the messiah. It is the scribes who speak about the "Christ," though Jesus quotes their thesis. Mark 13:21 speaks of pseudo-prophets coming after Easter and claiming to be the Christ, and Luke 24:26, 46 are words of the risen Lord, not of the earthly Jesus.

56 Quite a number of scholars think that verse 33 was the immediate reply of Jesus to the confession of Peter: "Get behind me, Satan! For you are not on the side of God, but of men." This seems to be highly improbable, for what group in the church would ever have handed down this piece of tradition? There is some trend in the Johannine literature to emphasize that "the disciple whom Jesus loved" was equal to Peter. Paul would say the same of himself, and Acts may, in some way, corroborate that. But nowhere do we find any evidence for a real fight against Peter within the early, pre-Markan church.

57 Cf. E. Käsemann, "Das Problem des historischen Jesus," *ZThK* 51, 1954, 125–153, also reprinted in his *Exegetische Versuche und Besinnungen* I, Göttingen, 1970, 200–212; furthermore, E. Schweizer, *Jesus Christus im vielfaltigen Zeugnis des Neuen Testamentes,* 5th ed., Gutersloh, 1979, 18–54 (English: *Jesus,* Richmond, 1971, [Atlanta, 1981, paperback] 13–51).

58 J. Jeremias, *Neutestamentliche Theologie* I, Gutersloh, 1971, 67–73 (English: *New Testament Theology* I, New York, 1971, 61–68).

59 Cf. the excursus in E. Schweizer, "Das Evangelium nach Markus" in *Das Neue Testament Deutsch* (vol. I), Göttingen, 1967 (English: *The Good News According to Mark,* Atlanta, 1970), to Mark 8:27–33, and in *Jesus Christus* (note 56), 22–26 (English: *Jesus,* 18–22). Cf. also N. Perrin, *Rediscovering the Teaching of Jesus,* New York, 1967, especially 164–173, 197–199, and for a corporate meaning of "Son of man" idem, *Jesus and the Language of the Kingdom: Symbol and Metaphor in New Testament Interpretation,* Philadelphia, 1976, 59.

60 The similitudes of Enoch have not been found in Qumran, whereas fragments of every other chapter of this collection of different writings have been detected. Some scholars date them in the second century A.D. But even if they were of pre-Christian origin, they are no safe basis. In "Menschensohn und eschatologischer Mensch im Fruhjudentum" (in *Jesus der Menschensohn,* A. Vogtle, ed. R. Pesch, Freiburg, 1975), 100–116, I have investigated a pre-Christian part of Ethiopic Enoch with the result that the most interesting references to "a man" (with exactly the same shift from man in general in the sense of *anthropos* to man as male in the sense of *aner* as in the Son of man passages of the similitudes) were missing in the Aramaic fragments and came only into the text by the Greek or even the Ethiopic translator (who were probably Christians). This should render us extremely cautious when we deal with evidence of texts out of Ethiopic Enoch, the translation of the translation of which we possess without even knowing whether the original had been written before the time of the New Testament.

61 Once on the Fiji Islands I met some students who were convinced that my view was the right one and even had good argu-

ments in favor of this thesis. However, I detected that they were so convinced because a visiting professor had told them so a few months before I came. So at least some students of the New Testament think so. I myself am not convinced of it beyond any doubts.

62 J. Drury, *Tradition and Design in Luke's Gospel,* Darton, Longman and Todd, 1976/John Knox, Atlanta, 1977, esp. pp. 1–6, 30–31, 174–175, 138–156, tries to show, in a challenging and stimulating book, that the Third Gospel is a midrash which develops Mark, and probably also Matthew, in the light of the Old Testament, especially of Deuteronomy, almost without any other sources. This would be, according to Drury, very much like the way in which 1/2 Chronicles rewrite the books of Samuel and Kings or Josephus, Philo, the Genesis Apocryphon and Jubilees parts of the Old Testament. In a similar way Domer (note 33) understands most of the new Lucan material as his own creation in the light of the Old Testament. Domer also compares Luke's method in the Gospel with the one used in Acts, as J.B. Tyson, *Source Criticism of the Gospel of Luke,* in C.H. Talbert (ed.), *Perspectives on Luke-Acts,* Danville, Va., and Edinburgh, 1978, p. 39, suggests. The problem of sources is difficult to solve since we are also not sure about the use of sources in Acts. Personally I think that Luke owes much of his new material to special sources, since in very many of the stories and parables peculiar to him sutures between tradition and Lucan interpretation are still detectable, though it is impossible to be sure about one's results in this field. For our purpose, however, it is not of first importance to know how far Luke's new understanding is or is not influenced by special sources which were at his disposal.